DATE DUE

DATE DUE			
OCT 1 0			
OCT 6			
NOV 0 1 1996			
NOV 0 2 1996			
GAYLORD			PRINTED IN U.S.A.

To the Hebrew Congregation in Newport
Rhode Island.

Gentlemen.

   While I receive, with much satisfaction,
your Address replete with expressions of affection
and esteem; I rejoice in the opportunity of assuring
you, that I shall always retain a grateful remem-
brance of the cordial welcome I experienced in
my visit to Newport, from all classes of citizens.

   The reflection on the days of difficulty and
danger which are past is rendered the more sweet,
from a consciousness that they are succeeded by days
of uncommon prosperity and security. If we have
wisdom to make the best use of the advantages with
which we are now favored, we cannot fail, under the
just administration of a good Government, to become
a great and a happy people.

   The citizens of the United States of America
have a right to applaud themselves for having given
to mankind examples of an enlarged and liberal
policy: a policy worthy of imitation. All possess
alike liberty of conscience and immunities of
citizenship. It is now no more that toleration is
spoken of, as if it was by the indulgence of one
class of people, that another enjoyed the exercise
of their inherent natural rights. For happily
the

the Government of the United States, which gives to bigotry no sanction, to persecution no assistance requires only that they who live under its protection should demean themselves as good citizens, in giving it on all occasions their effectual support.

It would be inconsistent with the frankness of my character not to avow that I am pleased with your favorable opinion of my administration, and fervent wishes for my felicity. May the children of the Stock of Abraham, who dwell in this land, continue to merit and enjoy the good will of the other Inhabitants; while every one shall sit in safety under his own vine and figtree, and there shall be none to make him afraid. May the father of all mercies scatter light and not darkness in our paths, and make us all in our several vocations useful here, and in his own due time and way everlastingly happy.

G.º Washington

THE
GOLDEN
DOOR

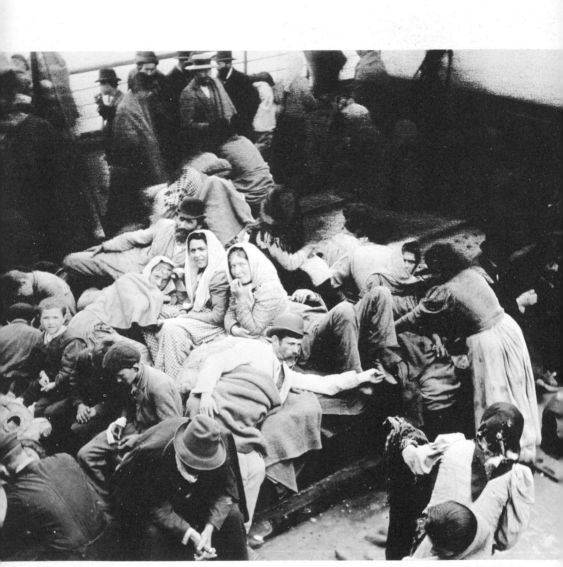

Immigrants coming to America aboard the *S. S. Westerland*, from a T. H. McAllister Company glass slide.

THOMAS J. FLEMING

THE GOLDEN DOOR

THE STORY OF AMERICAN IMMIGRATION

A W · W · NORTON BOOK
PUBLISHED BY
GROSSET & DUNLAP, INC.

Page   5:   *Western Star* by Stephen Vincent Benet
             Holt, Rinehart and Winston, Inc.
             Copyright 1943, by Rosemary Carr Benet
             Reprinted by permission of Brandt & Brandt.
Page 49:   The quote of the Norwegian immigrant, describing his decision to
             enlist from: *Foreigners in the Union Army and Navy* by Ella
             Lonn. Reprinted by permission of Louisiana State University Press.

Library of Congress Catalog Card Number: 74–105732
Copyright © 1970 by Thomas J. Fleming
Published simultaneously in Canada.
Printed in the United States of America.

To my four Irish immigrant grandparents
Bridget Green and David Fleming
Mary Fitzmaurice and Thomas Dolan

OTHER BOOKS BY THOMAS J. FLEMING

First in Their Hearts:
A Biography of George Washington

Affectionately Yours, George Washington:
A Self-Portrait in Letters of Friendship

One Small Candle:
The Pilgrims' First Year in America

CONTENTS

ILLUSTRATIONS

The port of LeHavre, France, photographed in 1851, was one of the many ports in Europe from which ships set sail with immigrants for America.

❧1❦

EARLY
ARRIVALS

In 1748, sixteen-year-old George Washington made his first
trip over Virginia's Blue Ridge mountains to work as a surveyor along the western frontier. One day he noted in his
journal meeting an Indian war party, homeward bound with
two scalps—and later a group of immigrants who impressed
the future father of his country as "ignorante . . . they would
never speak English but when spoken to they speak all
Dutch."

This offhand sentence sums up the story of the immigrant
in America. The young man who made the observation was the
great-grandson of immigrants who had been driven to Virginia
by poverty and religious persecution less than ninety years before. The immigrants who spoke only "Dutch" were Germans, seeking refuge on the frontier for almost identical
reasons.

So it has gone, from generation to generation. Each new
wave of immigrants has come to America poor and unschooled

and prospered until they came to regard the next wave as "ignorante." (Later generations added such unlovely names as *mick, wop, yid, polack, spik.*) Joseph P. Kennedy once remarked, "I was born in the United States and so was my father. Yet my children are still called Irish. What do we have to do to become American?" His son, John F. Kennedy, wanted to stop once and for all this futile pattern. When he died he was working on a book which he called *A Nation of Immigrants.*

It is the plain truth. All of us, from Mayflower descendants to the toddlers born to Cuban refugees from Castro's communism, are children of immigrants. President Franklin D. Roosevelt threw those haughty ancestor-worshippers, the Daughters of the American Revolution, into a furor when he reminded them of it. "Remember," he said in a 1938 speech, "remember always that all of us, and you and I especially, are descended from immigrants and revolutionists."

But the whole truth is larger than this plain truth. The story of American immigration is also one of the great sagas in the history of the human race. Since 1607, when the first English settlers landed at Jamestown, Virginia, a staggering forty-two million people have migrated to the United States— the largest mass movement in all recorded history.

Who were they—and why did they come? One thing is certain. From the beginning, almost to a man and woman, they were *not* aristocrats. Although there were a number of "gentlemen" among the first settlers in Virginia, they were of the poorer sort. As one of Virginia's earliest historians, Robert Beverely, remarked in 1705, "It is not likely that any man of a plentiful estate should voluntarily abandon a happy certainty to roam after imaginary advantages in a new world . . . the chief design of all parties was to fetch away . . . treasure."

MUSEUM OF THE CITY OF NEW YORK

Immigrants at Ellis Island, about 1907. Photo by Burt G. Phillips.

A replica of the flagship *Susan Constant II.* The original ship sailed to Jamestown from England in 1606 with the *Godspeed* and *Discovery*, bringing the first permanent English colonists to America.

Virginia's first marriage (1608) was between Ann Burras, a lady's maid, and John Laydon, a laborer. Stephen Vincent Benet describes the scene with fine irony in his narrative *Western Star.*

And the first white wedding held on Virginia ground
Will marry no courtly dame to a cavalier
But Ann Burras, lady's maid, to John Laydon, laborer.
After some six weeks' courtship—a Fall wedding
When the leaves were turning red and the wild air sweet
And we know no more than that, but it sticks in the mind
For they were serving maid and laboring man . . .
And yet, while they lived (and they had not long to live)
They were half of the first families of Virginia.

In New England, the story was much the same. There was not an iota of blue blood aboard the old freighter *Mayflower.* Nor, indeed, could any colony boast that its original settlers were the cream of European nobility. On the contrary, paupers and vagrants often signed on as indentured servants. Moreover, in 1717, Parliament decided to ease the overcrowding in British prisons by deporting convicted felons to America. Some fifty thousand of these criminals arrived in the colonies in the years before the Revolution.

The myth of aristocracy is not the only one that needs exploding. Because America is an English-speaking country, most of us have the impression that English immigrants alone cleared the forest primeval, fought the Revolution, secured independence—and then the "others"—Poles, Irish, Germans, Jews—began to arrive. Actually, most of America was well on its way to becoming a "nation of nations" by the time the embattled farmers fired the first shot at Lexington, Massachusetts, in 1775.

As early as September 25, 1608, six sturdy laborers strode ashore at Jamestown and within three weeks had a roaring fire going under a glass furnace, the first factory in America. Their names were Mical Lowicki, Zbigniew Stefanski, Jur Mata, Jan Bogdan, Karol Zrenica, and Stanislaw Sadowski. The enterprising sextet also organized a soap works, built a sawmill, and won high praise from no less an authority than Captain John Smith. The majority of the adventurers in his company, Smith declared were "ten times more fit to spoil a commonwealth, than either to begin one or to help maintain one." Most of them, he complained, "never did know what a day's work was, except the Dutchmen and Poles and some dozen others."

Some years later in 1619, when Virginia convened America's first representative assembly, Governor George Yeardley decreed that only natives of England would be allowed to vote. The Poles called the first strike in America's history and won an almost instant victory. The Court Book of the Virginia Company records: "Upon some dispute of the Polonians . . . it was now agreed that they shall be enfranchised and made as free as any inhabitant whatsoever."

The Poles' talent for hard work guaranteed them a welcome in almost every colony in the fledgling nation. Nieuw Amsterdam's Governor Peter Stuyvesant was always petitioning Dutch officials to send more Polish settlers to his island trading post. Among those who came was Dr. Alexander Kurcyusz, who became a teacher of Latin and Greek in one of the colony's earliest schools. Olbracht Zaborowski, an Indian trader, bought a large tract of land on the opposite side of the Hudson River. Zaborowski, who later shortened his name to Zabriskie, was one of New Jersey's earliest judges, and many of his descendants are still prominent in that state.

Another trader, Jan Antoni Sadowski, became Jonathan

Sandusky in the New World. His dealings with the Indians took him inland beyond the Alleghenies, and in 1735 he set up a trading post on Lake Erie. It is now the city of Sandusky, Ohio.

Nieuw Amsterdam was the first major colony to be established under non-British sponsorship. Its origins were unmistakably Dutch but its citizens came from all over Europe. One visitor to the colony reported that Italian, Swedish, Spanish, French—as many as eighteen different languages—were to be heard on the streets.

In 1654 twenty-three Jews, refugees from Portuguese persecution in Brazil, arrived in Nieuw Amsterdam. One of them, Asser Levy, won the first clear-cut victory for religious freedom in the New World. When he applied for citizenship in the Dutch colony, the governor, irascible Peter Stuyvesant, turned him down. For three years, Levy conscientiously performed all the duties of a citizen. He paid his taxes faithfully and regularly mounted guard along with the Dutch. Finally he reapplied, and by this time the burghers backed him so firmly that Stuyvesant was forced to grant him citizenship—though he warned that this would mean men of all religions would now be able to demand the same rights. This is exactly what happened. When the English took possession of the colony in 1664, they found almost as many religions as there were nationalities.

Jews, mostly refugees from Spain and Portugal often called Sephardic Jews, were to be found in other cities besides New York. They established congregations in Philadelphia; Newport, Rhode Island; and Charleston, South Carolina. Newport had a number of distinguished Jewish families and soon became a center of Hebrew culture. America's first synagogue was erected there. Financed by the contributions of Jews in all parts of the thirteen colonies, it was officially dedicated in 1763.

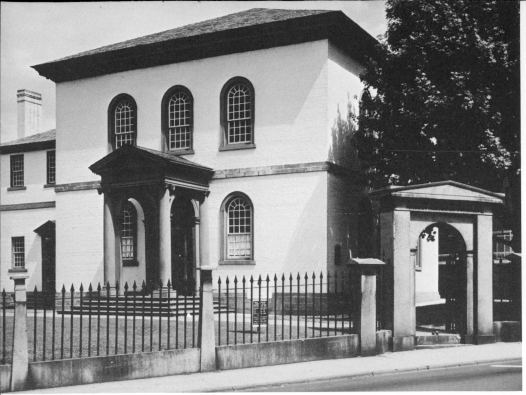

Touro Synagogue in Newport, Rhode Island. The Jewish community in Newport dates back to 1658. The synagogue was dedicated December 2, 1763.

Nels Wickstrom and his family posed for an unknown photographer in front of their log house in Florence County, Wisconsin, in 1893.

The synagogue still stands on Newport's Touro Street and is considered an architectural gem.

Elsewhere along the Atlantic seaboard, the influx of immigrants continued. A group of five hundred Swedes and Finns arrived in Delaware in 1638 and founded Fort Christina on the site of what is now the city of Wilmington. It was these sturdy planters who introduced that symbol of American pioneering, the log cabin.

Like most of the non-English arrivals, the Swedes were determined to adopt the principal language of their new country. Peter Kalm, a Swedish botanist who wrote an early account of colonial life, noted that the Swedes were ashamed to talk in their own tongue lest they not be considered "real English." "It is easy to see," he said, "that the Swedish language is doomed to extinction in America."

William Penn, in an effort to find colonists for his Quaker settlement, had published pamphlets describing its virtues in German, French, and Dutch. Although the advertisements attracted immigrants from all three countries, by far the majority were Germans—refugees from religious wars in the Rhineland. They poured into Pennsylvania in such numbers that in 1766 Benjamin Franklin estimated that the colony was one-third German. Ten years later, a census revealed they were 150,000 strong.

The earliest group arrived in 1683 under the leadership of Francis Daniel Pastorius. They established a settlement on a tract of land just north of Penn's City of Brotherly Love and called it, appropriately, Germantown. The new village soon became known for its farms and gardens and was also famous for the weaving of flax.

Many of the settlers eventually moved on to Delaware, Maryland, and farther west in Pennsylvania, to the area around

Lancaster County. Their farms were invariably the best managed and the most productive in the region, and their owners
never hesitated to hitch up their sturdy Conestoga wagons to
haul vegetables, meat, and fruits to even the most distant town
markets. These covered carts were the ancestors of the prairie
schooners that would later forge their way across the continent.

From France came the Huguenots, Protestants whose religious and political beliefs had made them outcasts from their
homeland. Some settled in South Carolina, where their family
names—Huger, Gaillard, Laurens—are still common. Pennsylvania, too, had its French citizens, and in New York, the Vas-
sars, Gallaudets, and Delanos (from De La Noye) claimed the
same ancestry.

Perhaps the largest influx of Huguenots arrived in the
colonies in 1689, after the destruction of their fortress, La
Rochelle. They founded the city of New Rochelle in New
York's Westchester County. The French were admired for
their talent as teachers and New Rochelle soon became famous
as an educational center. Wealthy New Yorkers sent their sons
there to learn French and their daughters to be schooled in
music, painting, and needlework.

In Virginia, French winemaking, weaving, and dressmaking
were so highly regarded that when some of the settlers moved
on to North Carolina, the Virginia Board of Trade furiously
complained that they had been lured away by their neighbors
to the south.

The ships that carried German and French passengers invariably included some Swiss as well. The earliest arrival appears to have been William Faldoe, a woodworker who was
recruited by the Virginia Company in 1608. Eventually, other
Swiss also arrived in the colony and were welcomed for their
thrift and hard work. "I had much rather do with the honest

Switzers," Governor William Byrd declared, "than the mixed people that come from Pennsylvania."

The predominately English Carolina Company hired a Swiss, Peter Fabian of Berne, as a surveyor and scientific adviser. The expedition also included twenty families from the Swiss canton of Vaud. The region is still famous as the heart of Switzerland's wine country, and its citizens hoped to produce the same commodity in the New World. A Swiss baron, Christopher de Graffenried, led the group of immigrants from his own country and Germany who founded New Bern, North Carolina in 1710. There were also some Swiss among the settlers who arrived in South Carolina to set up a silk industry in 1726.

The Irish, particularly the Protestants from the northern counties, streamed into American ports from Boston to Charleston in steady numbers. It has been estimated that by 1660, some ten thousand Irish had settled in various sections of the American colonies. They continued to be joined by their countrymen at such a rate that a hundred years later, Irish immigrants totaled ten thousand a year. Famed for their fighting prowess, the Irish were sought by every colony to serve as guards against the Indians along the frontier. Worcester, Massachusetts, and Londonderry, New Hampshire, are among some five hundred towns they founded on the edge of the wilderness.

Thousands of doughty Scots, Highlanders and Lowlanders, were welcomed for similar reasons and moved into the back country of Virginia and North and South Carolina. The earliest Scotch settler, David Thomson, founded the town of Rye, New Hampshire, and generously came to the rescue of the Pilgrims in Plymouth when their food and supplies were running short.

Other Scots settled in Pennsylvania, North and South Carolina, and blazed trails into Kentucky and Tennessee. Stern believers in the virtues of a classical education, Scotch Presbyterians were quick to establish schools wherever they went. Among them was the College of New Jersey, now known as Princeton, which was founded in 1746. Although not the earliest institution of higher learning in the country, it was the first to enroll students from all of the thirteen colonies.

Almost as important was another group of immigrants from the British Isles—the Welsh. Like the Scots and the Irish, they were under English rule, and many of them saw coming to America as an opportunity to revive Welsh nationalism, far from the heavy hand of London. Late in the 1600's, a group of Welshmen acquired a huge tract of land west of Philadelphia, some forty thousand acres, which became known as "the Welsh Barony." Welsh Quakers also settled in Pennsylvania, and many of the town names—Gwynnyd, Bryn Mawr—testify to their sturdy pride in their Welsh heritage. Soon there were enough Welshmen in Pennsylvania to justify publishing books in the Welsh language, and in many of these towns church services and legal documents were in Welsh for several generations. The use of the Welsh language gradually died out, but the Welsh *wynnestay*—a big, comfortable home, far larger than the ordinary pioneer cabin—inspired later generations to build the spacious Pennsylvania colonial farmhouse. The Welsh were considered highly desirable immigrants, and Maryland was one of several colonies that tried to attract Welsh farmers within their boundaries. Like their Scots cousins, they made excellent lawyers and were tough soldiers as well.

All of these immigrants to America came voluntarily, eager to take the risks and seize the opportunities of this rich, unexplored continent. But one group of immigrants did not come

An 1870 engraving of steerage passengers. The majority of immigrants to America crossed the Atlantic in accommodations similar to these.

of their own free will—the Negroes from Africa. In 1619, a year before the *Mayflower* landed its famous passengers in Plymouth, a Dutch ship deposited twenty Negroes at Jamestown, Virginia. We know the names of only a few—Anthony —Isabella—Pedro. Anthony is said to have fallen in love with Isabella and married her, and in 1624 she gave birth to the first Negro child born in English America. By 1710, there were fifty thousand Negroes toiling in the fields and houses of Virginia, Maryland, New Jersey, and almost every other English colony. Almost all were slaves, often captured by other Negroes in Africa, and sold on the coasts to slave traders, who in turn sold them to ship captains, who carried them to the New World. Branded and chained, they were packed like books on shelves into the holds of these slave ships with "not so much room," one captain said, "as a man in his coffin, either in length or breadth." Thousands died on the six- to ten-week voyage.

Although none of the voluntary immigrants endured living conditions as dreadful as those on the slave ships, by no stretch of the imagination could accommodations in the old sailing ships be described as luxurious. Sleeping space was so limited that it was hailed as a major reform when, in 1749, Pennsylvania passed a law decreeing that every immigrant over the age of fourteen should be provided with a berth six feet long and a foot and a half wide. It was another seventeen years before an equally important dimension—height—was taken into account. Then it was ruled that berths should be at least three feet nine inches apart in the forward parts of the ship. Two feet nine was considered adequate for steerage passengers.

But discomfort was a minor problem compared to danger. A boatload of 250 Swiss who sailed for Virginia in 1738 was shipwrecked and less than a dozen of the would-be immigrants escaped with their lives. Death from starvation and thirst was commonplace. Passengers were expected to supply their own food but the rations could easily spoil or run out if the ship was becalmed or had to stop for repairs.

Diseases—yellow fever, dysentery, and smallpox—were another threat, and it was a rare expedition that did not include at least one burial at sea. One voyage from Ireland counted seventy-five passengers dead before the ship reached port. On another ship, the toll was three hundred.

Nevertheless, the immigrants came—English, Germans, Poles, Dutch, Irish, Jews. They became Virginians, New Yorkers, Rhode Islanders. Out of this assortment of nationalities and cultures would emerge a new country whose citizens would proudly call themselves Americans.

⇜2⇝

MANY
FOUNDING FATHERS

WHEN THE THIRTEEN COLONIES bravely drew up their
Declaration of Independence, one of the grievances they cited
in it was George III's attempt to interfere with the influx of
non-English citizens. "He has endeavoured to prevent the population of these states;" they charged, "for that reason obstruct-
ing the laws for the Naturalization of Foreigners; refusing to
pass others to encourage their migrations hither, and raising
the condition of new Appropriations of Lands."

These "foreigners" played a vital role in the struggle to make
freedom a reality. Of the fifty-six signers of the Declaration of
Independence, eighteen were of non-English stock and eight
were first-generation immigrants. Thomas Jefferson borrowed
the phrase "All men are created equal" from the writings of his
friend Phillip Mazzei, a brilliant Italian who lived for a number of years in Virginia. Patrick Henry, one of the first to raise
his voice against British oppression, was descended from Scotch
Presbyterians who had settled in the back country of Virginia.

Charles Thomson, the man who recorded the most precious moments in American history as secretary of the Continental Congress, was born in County Derry, Ireland.

Peter Faneuil, a Boston merchant, descendant of French Huguenots, gave his native city the public meetinghouse that became famous as the "cradle of liberty." Another patriot, Paul Revere, was the son of an immigrant goldsmith, Apollos Revoire de Romagnieu.

Henry Laurens, one of the leading merchants of Charleston, South Carolina, was also of Huguenot ancestry. Laurens served as president of the Continental Congress in 1777–78. A year later, he set sail for Holland, where he hoped to arrange a treaty of friendship as well as a loan for the beleaguered colonies. His ship was captured by the British, and Laurens spent the next fifteen months imprisoned in the Tower of London "on suspicion of high treason." He was released after the battle of Yorktown in exchange for Lord Cornwallis and helped negotiate the treaty that finally granted America her independence. Laurens' son, John, an aide-de-camp to General Washington, was killed in one of the closing skirmishes of the Revolution.

As president of the Continental Congress in 1783, Elias Boudinot had the honor of signing the peace treaty with England. Boudinot, whose great-grandfather had emigrated from France in 1685, served as commissary general of prisoners during the Revolution and personally contributed thirty thousand dollars for their care.

Two Polish soldiers, Thaddeus Kosciuszko and Casimir Pulaski, played major roles in the American Revolution. Colonel Kosciuszko served as an engineer with the American Army and helped plan and build the defenses around West Point. Pulaski, a cavalryman, fought in a number of engage-

Phillip Mazzei.

NEW YORK PUBLIC LIBRARY

Casimir Pulaski. The Pulaski Skyway in New Jersey now bears his name.

NATIONAL ARCHIVES

ments and died a few days after being shot during a charge at Savannah, Georgia. Pulaski's legion included at least a dozen Polish soldiers who had come with him to America. Other Poles already living in the colonies were also to be found in the continental ranks. Among the Polish names on the muster rolls of Massachusetts were thirty men named Laski from the towns of Marblehead and Salem.

At times more than a third of the American army was Irish. The Pennsylvania line, one of Washington's toughest brigades, was often called "the line of Ireland." In the first months of the war, when the New England troops tried to celebrate Guy Fawkes Day, a notoriously anti-Catholic observance, General George Washington sternly rebuked them for planning such an insult to the Irish soldiers who fought beside them.

The New Englanders raised Irish tempers again at Valley Forge by parading a "stuffed Paddy"—a very uncomplimentary image of St. Patrick—around the camp. The Irish seized their muskets and for a moment it looked as if a civil war might erupt. But Washington quickly appeared and asked the Irish to point out their tormentors so he could have them punished. When the Irish declined to do so, Washington said: "Well, I too am a lover of St. Patrick, and must settle the affair by making all the army keep the day." Whereupon he ordered an extra ration of rum for every man in camp, and in the words of one of his aides, "All made merry and were good friends."

There is a gravestone in Virginia's Shenandoah Valley that reads:

Here lies the remains of John Lewis, who slew the Irish lord, settled in Augusta County, located the town of Staunton and furnished five sons to fight the battles of the American Revolution.

The Butler brothers of Lancaster, Pennsylvania, sons of a Dublin immigrant, served with distinction in the Continental Army. Captain Thomas Butler was in almost every major engagement of Washington's forces and won high praise for covering his brother Richard's retreat at the battle of Monmouth.

Major General John Sullivan was the son of a schoolteacher from County Limerick in Ireland. Commodore John Barry, the "father of the American Navy," was born in Tacumshane, Ireland. Major General Stephen Moylan, son of a prosperous Catholic merchant from Cork, served as Washington's secretary and later as quartermaster general to the Continental Army. One of the heroes of the victory at Princeton, the jovial Moylan was also on hand for the closing operations of the Yorktown campaign. Moylan's favorite uniform included buckskin breeches, a bearskin hat, a red waistcoat, and—undoubtedly out of loyalty to his homeland—a bright-green coat. When Moylan was elected first president of the Friendly Sons of St. Patrick, he promptly installed his friend George Washington as an honorary member.

When the British came charging up the slope at Bunker's Hill, one wing was led by a tough marine major named John Pitcairn. In the American redoubt, a Negro sharpshooter named Peter Salem, ignoring musket balls and cannon fire, thrust his long musket over the earthen wall and cut Pitcairn down with a single shot. Peter Salem was only one of at least five thousand Negroes who served in the Continental Army during the Revolution. Thousands more fought in the American militia. There were over 700 Negroes among the 13,500 Americans at the battle of Monmouth, where the Continentals slugged the British to a standstill. Massachusetts, Connecticut, and Rhode Island raised Negro units, which repeatedly distinguished

NATIONAL ARCHIVES

Major General Stephen Moylan.

themselves on the battlefield. But most of the black Americans fought beside white men as "integrated" soldiers. One enemy officer wrote: "No [American] regiment is to be seen in which there are not Negroes in abundance; and among them are able-bodied, strong and brave fellows."

THE NEW-YORK HISTORICAL SOCIETY, NEW YORK CITY

"Battle of Bunker's Hill, June 17, 1775." An 1808 engraving by James Mitan after the painting by John Trumbull depicting the historic battle. The black soldier in the extreme right-hand corner may well be Peter Salem.

The Jewish Cemetery on Pearl Street in New York City. This photograph was taken in 1905, and the cemetery dates back to Revolutionary days.

The chief financier of the Revolution was Robert Morris. Less well known but at least as devoted to the cause was his friend Haym Salomon, a Polish Jew who spent two years spying for the Americans in British-held New York, and then moved to Philadelphia, where he consumed his personal fortune advancing cash to congressmen, army officers, and the bankrupt American government. James Madison wrote home: "The kindness of our little friend on Front Street near the coffee house is a fund that will preserve me from extremities, but I never resort to it without mortification for he obstinately rejects all recompense."

Other Jews fought in the revolutionary ranks. An early Jewish cemetery on the edges of New York's Chinatown contains the graves of some fifteen veterans of the War for Independence. Solomon Pinto was one of the original members of Connecticut's Society of the Cincinnati, an organization composed of Revolutionary War officers.

Swiss immigrants, bred in a centuries-old tradition of liberty, were quick to champion independence in their new homeland. The Reverend John Zubly represented Georgia at the Continental Congress. Henry Wisner was active in forming the Committees of Safety in New York. After the British clamped down on the colonial importation of gunpowder, Wisner established his own powder mill in Goshen, New York. A member of the Continental Congress, he was an outspoken supporter of the proposed Declaration of Independence and might have become one of its signers. By the summer of 1776, however, he was home in Goshen supervising the production of desperately-needed ammunition for the American troops.

John Jacob Faesch, an immigrant from Basle, Switzerland, produced revolutionary cannonballs by the thousands at his ironworks in Ringwood, New Jersey. And in Lancaster, Pennsylvania, Martin Meylin, another Swiss, founded America's first boring mill, where he trained the Swiss and German gunmakers who supplied many of the weapons used in the defense of the colonies. The long-range Pennsylvania rifles they turned out proved to be so effective that at one point in the war, Parliament ordered an investigation into "these strange arms used with such deadly certainty by American regiments."

Of all the Swiss who have left their mark on our nation's history, Albert Gallatin is undoubtedly the best known. Gallatin, a college student in Geneva at the time of the American revolution, abandoned his books and set out to enlist in the American army. His military career was a brief one. The war ended about the same time he arrived in America but Gallatin decided to remain anyway. He learned English while teaching French at Harvard, then left to settle on an estate in western Pennsylvania. He was elected to the state legislature and later to congress, but the high point of his career was his thirteen-year tenure (1800–1813) as secretary of the treasury under Presidents Jefferson and Madison.

The list of Germans who volunteered for service with the Continental Army is almost endless. The news of the battles of Lexington and Concord had barely reached Reading when the Germans there raised four companies of infantrymen. The German Fusiliers of Charleston were recruited in less than twenty-four hours. One of the most fiery German leaders was Peter Muhlenberg, the son of a Lutheran missionary who had come to America in 1742. The elder Muhlenberg sent his sons back to Germany for their education but Peter returned home after a few years, securing his passage by enlisting as secretary to one of the officers of a British regiment, the "Royal Americans." Discharged soon after his arrival, Muhlenberg decided to follow his father into the ministry and become pastor of a Lutheran church in Virginia's Shenandoah valley. In January, 1776, he ascended the pulpit and preached a blazing sermon to his German immigrant congregation. Taking his text from Ecclesiastes, he declared, "There is a time for preaching and praying but also a time for battle and that time has now arrived." Muhlenberg then flung aside his ministerial robes to reveal the uniform of an American colonel. Three hundred men enlisted at the church door. By 1777, Muhlenberg was a brigadier general. As he led his men into the battle of Brandywine, the German troops fighting as mercenaries on the British side recognized him and cried out, *"Hier kommt Teufel Pete"*— "here comes Devil Pete"—a nickname he had earned in his rowdy student days in Germany.

Baron Friedrich Wilhelm von Steuben, the Prussian drillmaster who whipped Washington's bedraggled recruits at Valley Forge into a working army, was probably the best-known German to join the fight for independence. The Baron, who spoke almost no English, used to fume at his untrained soldiers in German and French. When his ire reached its peak, he would turn to his aide, Captain Benjamin Walker, and have him continue the tirade in English. After the war von Steuben elected to stay in America. He was granted citizenship by a special act of the Pennsylvania legislature and settled in New York, where he lived until his death in 1794.

Another German hero was huge Johann Kalb, a Bavarian peasant who became a general in the Continental Army. The Baron de Kalb, as he was known in America, arrived as a soldier of fortune but soon became as dedicated to the cause of independence as the most sincere son of liberty. Against his advice, General Horatio Gates undertook the August, 1780, attack at Camden, South Carolina, which turned into one of the most disastrous American defeats of the entire war. Al-

NEW YORK PUBLIC LIBRARY

Baron de Kalb.

most a thousand Americans were killed or wounded in the battle, among them Kalb, who suffered eleven wounds in the fight and died three days later.

Nicholas Herkimer of upstate New York also won fame in the American Revolution. When the war began he organized four regiments, all with German colonels and largely German recruits. In 1777, when the British master plan for ending the war called for three armies to drive down New York State and cut the colonies in two, Herkimer was the first to meet the challenge.

In a fierce guerrilla encounter at Oriskany, he fought his way out of an ambush and, though mortally wounded, directed an all-day battle that eventually drove back the British and their Indian allies with heavy losses. It was a crucial victory and led directly to the British surrender at Saratoga, the turning point of the war. Washington paid tribute to the New Yorker, saying, "It was Herkimer who first reversed the gloomy scene . . . he served from love of country, not for reward."

Not all of the German help came in the lines of battle. Christopher Ludwig, a Pennsylvania baker, was appointed superintendent and director of baking for the entire Continental Army. It was a gargantuan assignment. Ludwig and his assistants often produced as many as six thousand loaves of bread a day.

Scotch names abounded in the revolutionary ranks. The most famous is certainly that of John Paul Jones, the American naval hero who was born in Kirkcudbrightshire, Scotland. Jones' reputation rests mainly on his daring capture of the British ship *Serapis* off the English coast in 1779. It was this feat which led King George III to denounce him as a "pirate . . . who is a rebel subject and a criminal of the state."

A less flamboyant but equally canny patriot was Henry Knox, who served as chief of artillery for the colonial forces. Knox counted as his ancestor the Laird of Gifford from the lowlands of Scotland. His father, William Knox, had migrated from his native land to Derry in northern Ireland and then to Boston. The younger Knox, owner of a Boston bookshop, had read a great deal about military affairs but his fighting experience was limited to volunteer service at the battle of Bunker Hill.

George Washington was appointed Commander-in-Chief soon after that battle and met Knox when he arrived in Cambridge to assume his new post. He was so impressed with the portly bookseller that he asked him to take charge of his yet-to-be-organized artillery. Knox remained in the post until the victory at Yorktown and later became our first secretary of war in Washington's cabinet.

America's quarrel with the mother country aroused the sympathy of several European nations, among them Holland. Dutch interest in the war accelerated after John Paul Jones brought the captured *Serapis* into one of their harbors as a prize of war. In Amsterdam, one group of sympathetic citizens loaded a warship with grain and sailed it through the British blockade to Baltimore as a gift to the beleaguered Americans.

Nor did the revolutionary army lack for soldiers of Dutch descent. Colonel Theunis Dey, commander of the rear guard that covered Washington's retreat across New Jersey, was descended from one of Peter Stuyvesant's soldiers. Dey commanded a company of his Bergen County neighbors, most of whom also boasted ties with Nieuw Amsterdam.

Other Dutch names appear in the official records. Phillip Van Cortlandt, Goose Van Schaick, Richard Varick, and Phillip Schuyler were officers of the Continental Army. Several thousand troops at the battle of Saratoga were Hudson Valley farmers who still spoke the Dutch of their fathers and grandfathers.

Among the heroines of the American struggle was Elizabeth Zane, daughter of Ebenezer Zane, the founder of Wheeling, West Virginia. Zane, of Danish origin, led the defense of Wheeling when it was attacked by the British in 1782. The settlers, huddled together in the log fort, were considerably outnumbered by the British and their Indian allies. Their powder supply was almost exhausted. There was a full keg in a small cabin some yards from the fort and young Elizabeth volunteered to get it. She slipped out of the gates, darted through the bullets, and returned with the keg supposedly concealed in her apron. The extra ammunition enabled Zane and his men to hold out until reinforcements arrived and scattered the attackers.

Another fighting frontiersman was the Italian Giuseppe Maria Francisco Vigo, who played a crucial role in the 1779 capture of Fort Vincennes, key to the northwest. Not only did he guide the American expedition across 240 miles of un-mapped winter wilderness; he put up most of the money for the food, equipment, and ammunition. One historian of the victory (which eventually brought the states of Ohio, Indiana, Illinois, Michigan, and Wisconsin, and part of Minnesota, into the union) declared: "The whole credit belongs to two men, General George Rogers Clark and Colonel Francis Vigo."

By the time the Revolutionary War ended, keen observers such as St. Jean de Crèvecoeur, a Frenchman who lived on a farm in Orange County, New York, were already noting that "here individuals of all nations are melted into a new race of men." To prove it, Crèvecoeur cited a family in his vicinity whose four sons were married to women of four different nationalities.

The administration of the new nation reflected this melting pot. John Hanson, temporary chief executive under the Articles of Confederation, was the grandson of one of the first settlers in Delaware's New Sweden. Alexander Hamilton, the master-mind of the U.S. banking system, was born in the West In-dies of a Scotch father and French mother. John Jay, our first chief justice, was the grandson of a New York Huguenot; his mother was a Dutch Van Cortlandt and he himself married the daughter of New Jersey's Governor William Livingston, whose ancestors were Scotch.

The leaders of the United States were determined to keep

this tradition of immigration alive. In December, 1783, Washington wrote a reply to an address from a group of recent arrivals from Ireland: "The bosom of America is open to receive not only the Opulent and respectable Stranger but the oppressed and persecuted of all Nations and Religions."

Thomas Jefferson echoed his sentiments a few years later when he asked: "Shall we refuse to the unhappy fugitives from distress that hospitality which the savages of the wilderness extended to our fathers arriving in this land? Shall oppressed humanity find no asylum on this globe?"

❧3❧

HERE COME
THE IRISH

In 1816 Thomas Wilson, United States consul in Dublin, wrote to Secretary of State James Monroe: "The principal freight from Ireland to the United States consists of passengers." The words signaled the beginning of the era of mass immigration. The Irish came first, prodded by crop failures and a desire to escape the heavy hand of the British government's Penal Laws, which refused Catholics the right to own land, and kept Ireland in a subjugated, colonial status. With thousands of their countrymen already established in America, it was inevitable that the desperately poor in Ireland's countryside would look to the New World as the answer to their misery. The Irish, said the British consul in Boston, regarded the United States "as a sort of half-way stage to Heaven."

As soon as the Napoleonic Wars were over, and the ocean was once more open to peaceful shipping, the Irish began their exodus. The tide mounted gradually at first, about twenty thousand a year in the early 1820's, hitting a high of ninety-

two thousand in 1842. They came on timber ships from
Canada, wallowing, three-masted tubs, prone to foundering.
Ships that carried coolies from Madras to the West Indies were
pressed into the trade. (An Irish member of Parliament sarcas-
tically suggested that emigrant ships ought to be at least as good
as the vessels used to transport convicts to Australia.) Some
even came on a *Mayflower*—from Ballyshannon. The fare was
between $12.50 and $25.00, and even this pittance was
usually borrowed from half the village. The average passenger
got no more than his breadth and length upon the deck of the
ship, with his sea chest for his bed. Dozens who could not afford the fare tried to ride free. While the ship was being towed
from the dock out into the stream to begin the Atlantic voyage,
the crew dug stowaways out of barrels and chests, from beneath
lifeboats and sails. One man, Martin Dooley, crept into the
provision locker and crouched there, his legs under him, for the
entire voyage. In Boston, they had to amputate both his legs.

From first to last, the immigrant ran a gauntlet of fellow
Irish "sharks" and "man-catchers" who specialized in swindling
him. They changed his money for foreign coins, worth less
than American dollars, and sold him bad food he would supposedly need on the voyage, as well as cheap cooking utensils,
at outrageous prices. Others told him that the shortest way to
America was the voyage to New Orleans, and forced him to pay
out of his tiny savings twice the fare to New York. A kindhearted
American captain described the immigrants as "a lot of sheep
surrounded by wolves." A British official complained that they
were "of the most simple and ignorant character; they will believe anything."

Still they came, braving and enduring the humiliations and
the frauds. By the mid-1840's over a million Irish had made
the difficult voyage. Then came that fateful day in 1845 when

INSPECTION CARD.

(IMMIGRANTS AND STEERAGE PASSENGERS.)

Port of Departure, CORK (QUEENSTOWN), IRELAND.　　Date of Departure,

Name of Ship, SCYTHIA.　　　　　　　　　　　　15 MAY 96

Name of Immigrant, ... Last residence, ...

Inspected and passed at ...

Passed at Quarantine, port of ... Boston ...

(Date.)

The following to be filled in by Ship's Surgeon or Agent prior to or after embarkation.)

Ship's List or Manifest ... No. on Ship's List or Manifest.

Berth No.

The inspection card of an Irish immigrant aboard the *Scythia*, bound from Cork, Ireland, to Boston, Massachusetts, in 1896.

early risers in Ireland noted a peculiar smell in the country air. Blight had struck the potato crop—the food of the poor. The Great Famine had begun. For five successive years the potatoes rotted in their beds, and over 1,500,000 Irish died of starvation or the diseases of malnutrition. Almost 2,000,000 others fled a land that had become a huge cemetery.

This tidal wave of despairing humanity burst on the shores of a startled America. The statistics themselves tell the story best. From May, 1847, when the New York Commissioners of Emigration started to keep records, until the end of 1860, 1,107,034 Irish cascaded into the port, three-fourths, or 715,291, in the peak years 1848–53. The grand total for all ports for the years 1840–60 was a staggering 1,694,838. By 1850, the Irish formed 44 percent of the foreign-born population of the United States.

They were poor, desperately, unbelievably poor. The stench of some of them, as they emerged from six to eight weeks in the foul steerages of the immigrant ships, caused proper Bostonians to vomit. In New York and other cities they crowded

Mulberry Bend, one of the original Five Points in New York City. This photograph was taken for the Board of Health in 1872 by Jacob A. Riis, who was himself an immigrant from Denmark.

into America's first slums. In the Five Points (now Foley Square) neighborhood of New York, the Irish, according to one eyewitness, "occupied the oldest most rickety wooden buildings, open to the wind and the storm and far less comfortable than the buildings used as barns or cattle stalls by the great body of farmers throughout the country." There were no toilets or sewers in these buildings. Even water had to be carted from outdoor pumps. The Broad Street section of Boston, a similar slum, was, with the exception of a few blocks of Liverpool, England, the most densely populated place in the western world. Lemuel Shattuck, a census statistician, estimated that the average lifespan of an Irish immigrant in Boston was fourteen years.

Thus the Irish bore the first bitter brunt of the "mass immigration" era. Inevitably, the grinding poverty of slum life broke the hearts and health of thousands. Every day in the Irish press there were pitiful advertisements inserted by wives calling for husbands to return to deserted families. From 1849–59, 85 percent of the foreign-born admitted to Bellevue Hospital were Irish. In a typical year, 55 percent of those arrested in New York were Irish. Gangs of Irish hoodlums, such as the Kerryonians, Swamp Angels, Slaughterhousers, Dead Rabbits, and Honeymooners terrorized the Five Points and Bowery sections of New York. One historian of the era wrote: "No human life was safe, and a well dressed man venturing into the district was commonly set upon and murdered or robbed or both before he had gone a block. . . . The Police would not march against the denizens of [the district] except in parties of a half dozen or more." Every evening the Honeymooners stationed a gangster at each corner of Madison Avenue and Twenty-ninth Street with orders to knock down and rob every well-dressed man who appeared. Few of these hoodlums were more than twenty years old. They were obviously products of a complete breakdown of the family and every other form of discipline in the chaotic slums.

But most of the crimes committed by the immigrants were the minor vices of the poor. A typical report from a New York newspaper of the day read:

> ARRESTS—*John McGorty and Michael Dowd were arrested for stealing a keg of white lead; John McKenney on suspicion of having stolen $34; Jane Mullen for stealing a wash tub; Mary Donahan stole 34½ yards of calico from the premises of Mr. Taylor, 31 Catherine Street.*

Thousands upon thousands of other Irish fought the evil undertow of slum life. They worked, men and women both, almost all as laborers and servants in the beginning. With no skills beyond native wit and strength, they built America's canals and railroads, laid its sewers, toiled as serving maids to wealthier Americans. A laborer's pay, when he got it, was seldom more than $1.25 a day, and out of this meager sum he had to buy his food and clothing at stores run by the contractors who hired him. He worked from sunrise until, as one laborer put it, "our sweat mixes with the nightly dew."

Tyrone Power, ancestor of the late movie actor, sent home the following description of Irish laborers at work in Louisiana:

> *I only wish that wise men at home who cruelly charge the present condition of Ireland upon inherent laziness of her population could be transported to this spot [Louisiana], to look upon the hundreds of fine fellows laboring beneath the sun that at this winter season was at times insufferably fierce, and amidst a pestilential swamp whose exhalations were fetid to a degree scarcely endurable for a few mo-*

*ments; wading amidst stumps of trees, knee-deep in black
mud, clearing the spaces pumped out by powerful steam
engines; wheeling, digging, hewing or bearing burdens that
made one's shoulders ache to look upon; exposed, meantime,
to every change of temperature, in log huts laid down in
the very swamps on a foundation of newly felled trees.
Here they subsist on the coarsest fare, excluded from all
the advantages of civilization; often at the mercy of a hard
contractor who wrings his profits from their blood; and all
this for a pittance that merely enables them to exist. . . .*

One observer estimated that twenty-five out of every hundred
railroad workers died from causes connected with the work.
Again and again, contractors (most of them fellow Irish)
would abscond with the month's wages, which led to so-called
Irish-riots. At various times the militia of Baltimore, Chicago
and New York State had to be called out to stop enraged Irishmen from tearing up their own handiwork.

Out of their pitifully small wages, the Irish saved incredible
amounts of money which they sent home to bring friends and
families to America. The story of these Irish "remittances" was
to be repeated by subsequent immigrant groups. From 1848
to 1861, Irish immigrants sent home the known sum of $59,-
236,555. Other estimates for twenty years before the Civil
War reached $120,000,000. Nicholas Waterhouse, at a meet-
ing of English social scientists in 1858, declared: "If we look
back through the pages of American history to the day when the
Mayflower first sighted that wild New England shore, we shall
find no more magnificent spectacle than this—the work not of
the great, the rich or the mighty, but of those who were poor
and needy and destitute of all things have true hearts and strong
hands."

Unfortunately, people tend to see the worst in strangers—

and the Irish, with their brogues and quick tempers, their ragged clothes and Catholicism, were very strange to Americans. Thus the Irish became the first immigrants to feel the cruel lash of group prejudice.

George Washington and earlier Americans might have looked down on recent arrivals, but they never inflicted injuries on them or tried to bar their progress. But group prejudice aims at these ugly goals. In newspapers throughout the nation appeared advertisements such as the following: "WOMAN WANTED—to do general housework . . . English, Scotch, Welsh, German, or any country or color except Irish."

One day in 1857, George Templeton Strong, a wealthy New Yorker, happened upon an excavation where two Irish laborers had been killed in a cave-in. Here is how he described it in his diary:

> *They had just been dragged, or dug, out and lay white and stark on the ground where they had been working, ten or twelve feet below the level of the street. Around them were a few men who had got them out, I suppose, and fifteen or twenty Irish women, wives, kinfolk or friends who had got down there in some inexplicable way.*
>
> *The men were listless and inert enough, but not so the women. I suppose they were "keening" and altogether were raising a wild unearthly cry, half shriek and half song, wailing as a score of daylight banshees, clapping their hands and gesticulating passionately. Now and then one of them would throw herself down on one of the corpses, or wipe some trace of defilement from the face of the dead man with her apron, slowly and carefully, then resume her lament. It was an uncanny sound to hear, quite new to me.*
>
> *Our Celtic fellow citizens are almost as remote from us in temperament and constitution as the Chinese.*

Here is how the prejudiced editor of the *Chicago Post* described a typical Irishman: "Teddy O'Flaherty votes. He has not been in the country six months. He has hair on his teeth. He never knew an hour in civilized society. He is a born savage—as brutal a ruffian as an untamed Indian . . . the born criminal and pauper of the civilized world. To compare him with an intelligent freedman [a freed Negro slave] would be an insult to the latter. . . . The Irish fill our prisons and our poorhouses. Scratch a convict or a pauper and the chances are you tickle the skin of an Irish Catholic!"

Some Irish became convinced that there was no hope of winning acceptance from native Americans, and they proposed migrating to the far west, to set up a semi-independent nation within the United States. As early as 1818, Irish societies in the east were petitioning Congress for land grants "to build a new and happy Erin in the bosom of the West." Congress rejected the idea, fearing to turn America into "a patchwork nation."

This 1898 photograph by J. J. Pennell of the gravesite of Patrick Flanagan on the Kansas prairies shows dramatically the loneliness of life on the American Great Plains, which most Irish immigrants avoided. The inscription reads: "In memory of Patrick Flanagan, born County Roscommon, Ireland, Dec. 25, 1817, died Dec. 31, 1892."

REGIONAL HISTORY DEPARTMENT, KENNETH
SPENCER RESEARCH LIBRARY, UNIVERSITY OF KANSAS

Among the immigrants, the westward movement never caught on, anyway. The Irish did not like farming, especially on the vast lands of the American prairie. The life was too lonely. One who tried it complained: "Here everyone can get so much land . . . that they call them neighbors that lives two or three miles off." Sociable by nature, the Irishman preferred the city. Although they were crowded into ghettos, they soon realized that in America their sheer numbers made them count for something on election day. Moreover, the Irishman's natural talent with words—some called it "blarney" or "gab" —and his abundant natural charm made him a born politician. A poem written in 1838 makes fun of the dream of an Irish farming nation in the west, and at the same time underscores what the Irish saw as their real opportunity in America.

> *I tell ye not to leave the city*
> *Because ye know t'would be a pity*
> *To see men digging farms and doating*
> *Who should be in the city voting.*

Soon native Americans were complaining ominously about the dangers of "Irish power" in state and city governments. They combined this with a violent antipathy to the Irishman's Catholic religion, the traditional foe of Protestantism in Europe. Although the Irish had been fighting English exploitation before America was discovered, they were accused of being hostile to democracy. Even liberal Ralph Waldo Emerson suspected "the wild Irish element . . . led by Romanish priests who sympathize, of course, with despotism."

Before 1860, it was unusual to see Irishmen elected to anything beyond local office—alderman, sheriff, constable, perhaps mayor. Prejudice was so strong that native Americans regularly "scratched" any name on a ballot which began with an O or an *Mc*. As the Irish complained, "they put their mark on him who bore the name of Mc ———."

Gradually this hostility grew into a political movement, the Native American party, nicknamed the "Know-Nothings" because each member took a solemn oath to answer "I know nothing" to any inquiry from an outsider. Feeding on ignorance and anti-Catholicism, they ran candidates for public office who pledged to rid the country of foreign influence. In 1854 they elected six state governors and seventy-five congressmen and in 1856 won 25 percent of the presidential vote. Know-Nothing agitators took to street corner pulpits to denounce the Irish. "The Negro is black outside," they would shout, "the Irishman is black inside."

Sparked by such gutter attacks, ugly anti-Irish riots exploded in Philadelphia and New York. Mobs swarmed through Irish neighborhoods in Clinton and Southbridge, Massachusetts, burned a church in Raritan, and shot an Irishman to death in Newark, New Jersey. In Ellsworth, Maine, a priest was stripped, tarred and feathered, and left unconscious on a wharf. Sisters of Charity were assaulted on the streets of Providence, Rhode Island. A Know-Nothing mayor arrested the Irish-Catholic bishop of Pittsburgh on a trivial charge.

It is frightening to think of what the Know-Nothings might have done to the Irish and their fellow immigrants. But the movement collapsed because it could not agree on the great issue of the era—slavery. When the nation went to war to decide whether it would remain half slave and half free, the vast majority of Irish saw it as their opportunity to prove their questioned loyalty to the Republic.

An artist's interpretation of the departure of the 69th Regiment, New York State Militia (Fighting 69th) on April 23, 1861. From *Manual of the Corporation of the City of New-York,* 1862, by D. T. Valentine.

4

ALL FOR
THE UNION

THE BOSTON *Pilot* spoke for Irish-Catholic opinion in the north with its proclamation, "The Union—it must be preserved!" By careful count, 144,221 Irish-born soldiers swelled the Union ranks in response to that call. No fewer than thirty-eight regiments in the Union army had the word *Irish* in their names. The Ninth Massachusetts Regiment was known as "the Irish Ninth." The Nineteenth Illinois, led by Colonel Timothy O'Meara, was called the Irish Legion. Most famous of all the Gaelic units was the Irish Brigade, five regiments largely recruited in New York City by Thomas Francis Meagher, a noted patriot exiled by the British.

Almost as well known was the Sixty-ninth New York Regiment, described by one prejudiced war correspondent as composed of "strolling drunken vagabonds . . . picked up in the low groggeries of New York." But this same reporter admitted they "fought like tigers" at the battle of Bull Run. They were soon known as the Fighting Sixth-ninth, a title which they were to bear proudly through the wars of the twentieth century. More than a few of these Irish regiments went into battle with green flags flying beside the Stars and Stripes. The flag of the Twenty-eighth Massachusetts featured a harp and a Gaelic inscription meaning "Clear the road."

At Antietam Creek, which flows into the Potomac near Sharpsburg, Maryland, the Irish Brigade achieved a terrible immortality. Five regiments—three from New York, one from Pennsylvania, and one from Massachusetts—held the center of the Union line. Opposite them the Confederates were entrenched along a sunken road, behind a breastwork of fence rails. Again and again other Union regiments had tried to assault this key to the Confederate battle line, only to fall back before the blizzard of fire from the southern muskets. Soon Bloody Lane, as the soldiers called it, became the focal point of the battle. Finally, the Irish Brigade was ordered to attack. Meagher rose in his stirrups and roared, "Follow me, boys. Follow me." Across the smoke-shrouded field the Irish plunged. Meagher's horse went down, flinging its rider headlong. But the shouting, cheering Gaels swept forward into the very muzzles of the Confederate guns and in the words of a watching Pennsylvania soldier, "The enemy, in irreparable confusion, broke for the friendly cover of the timber." The Brigade lost one-fourth of its officers and one-third of its men that day. No wonder George McClellan, the Union commanding general, thanked the Irish Brigade "for superb conduct in the field" and declared he wished he had "twenty thousand more of them."

Fredericksburg was another climax in the bitter history of the Irish Brigade. Six times they were ordered to assault the Confederate line on the high hill, known as Marye's Heights, just outside the little Virginia town. As they went into battle,

General Meagher heartened them with a uniquely Irish command, "Fellow exiles of Erin, the flags of our native land have been shot to pieces; the green color is all gone from them, but there is plenty of boxwood in the streets of Fredericksburg. Pluck it, place it in your hats and you'll fight for your adopted land beneath the immortal banner of green." Six times, with their favorite color to mark their ranks, they flung themselves at the impregnable Confederate position. At the end of that terrible day, there were only two hundred men left in the Irish Brigade. The correspondent of the *Times* of London wrote: "Never . . . was more undaunted courage displayed by the sons of Erin than in those six frantic dashes. . . . The bodies which lie in dense masses . . . are the best evidence of what manner of men they were who pressed on to death with the dauntlessness of a race which has gained glory on a thousand battlefields."

How the rest of the army regarded their heroism can be seen from a story told by a soldier from another regiment who joined the Irish in one of those hopeless charges. His chaplain said to him, "It must have been a great consolation to you in your hour of danger to have known that you were supported by Divine Providence."

The soldier replied, "We were supported by the Irish Brigade and that was consolation enough."

After Fredericksburg, when the Union battle line poised for attack, more than one general asked: "Are the green flags ready?"

The large number of Irish in the Union army brought Catholic chaplains into the service for the first time in an official capacity. Soon one of them, Father B. F. Christy, was declaring that a few years in the service would do more to wipe out bigotry than a century in civilian life. More than once these priests played a key role in heartening the Irish soldier. Father William Corby, the chaplain of the Irish Brigade, galloped down the line minutes before they charged at Antietam. He told the men to make an act of contrition and gave them all absolution for their sins. Within minutes, 506 of them were dead. A statue in memory of this Irish-American priest stands on Cemetery Ridge at Gettysburg, where he played no small part in encouraging the men of the brigade to beat back the last Confederate assault in that crucial battle, the turning point of the war.

Catholic women, too, followed their men into battle. One of the most famous was Sister Anthony of Limerick, a nun whom many called the Florence Nightingale of the Civil War. She led groups of nursing nuns into the battlefield hospitals to ease the terrible suffering of the wounded in an era when medicine lacked anesthesia and drugs to fight infections. After the war, two grateful non-Catholics built a hospital for this brave woman, in Cincinnati.

Almost as famous was Bridget Divers, or "Irish Biddy," as the soldiers called her, the wife of a private in the First Michigan Cavalry. She often did sentry duty with the men, and even rode out with them on scouting and raiding expeditions. Once, riding with a wagon train that was attacked by Confederate cavalry, she rallied the poorly armed teamsters and with her encouragement they fought off the southern raiders and made it safely into the Union camp. She regularly visited the Christian Commission to obtain books and papers for the men, asserting that she was "acting chaplain." She knew as much as any practicing physician of the day about the treatment of wounds and disease.

A colonel in a Pennsylvania regiment described another Irish woman in action:

She remained close to the side of her husband and refused to retire to a place of security. Occasionally she would notice some fellow sneaking to the rear when she would run after him, seize him by the nape of his neck, placing him in the ranks again, calling him a dirty, cowardly spalpeen, and other choice epithets. The flying shells had no terrors for her. During the hottest of the cannonade this courageous woman walked fearlessly about among the troops encouraging them to stand up to their work. Her only weapon, offensive or defensive, was a large umbrella she carried under her arm.

Off the battlefield, the Irish were not model soldiers. They frequently drank too much or were absent without leave, and more than a few were court-martialed for brawling with their own kind as well as with soldiers from other regiments.

Their ready wit often got them out of scrapes. One officer told of the time that an Irishman asked him for a furlough, explaining his wife was sick and there was no one to care for the children.

"Pat, that's very strange," the officer replied, "the chaplain has a letter from your wife asking us not to send you home. She says every time you go home on leave you get drunk and frighten the children."

"Faith," said Pat, "there's two of the most splendid liars in the army in this room. I was never married in me life."

Irishmen fought on the Confederate side too. There were nearly eighty-five thousand Irish in the South when the war began and an estimated forty thousand of them responded to the call of the Confederacy. "Everywhere in the Confederate states," the newspaper, *The Southern Watchman* of Athens, Georgia, "they (the Irish) have been among the foremost to volunteer." The Irish Tartars was a famous unit from Louisiana. The Emmet Guards and the Montgomery Guards were companies from Richmond, Virginia. At Fredericksburg, Georgia Irishmen were among the Confederates manning Marye's Hill when the Irish Brigade made its hopeless heroic charges. The Emerald Guards of the Eighth Alabama Regiment wore dark-green uniforms and carried a shamrock and harp emblazoned on one side of their Confederate flag. The chief engineer on the famous Confederate raider the *Alabama* was an Irishman, Michael Quinn.

One of the most famous southern commanders was Major General Patrick Cleburne. He was an impulsive, generous Irishman with remarkable oratorical gifts. As he went into battle at Franklin, Tennessee, in 1864, he saw a private struggling across the battlefield in bare, bleeding feet. Cleburne leaped from his horse and handed his boots to the private. "Here," he said, "you need them more than I do." A few minutes later he led his men against the well-entrenched Federal battle line in a daring charge that ended with his death.

The Irish were by no means the only immigrant group that volunteered in large numbers for the war. The Seventy-ninth Highlanders of New York were all Scottish at first, although eventually they sought Irishmen to fill their decimated ranks. They fought with ferocity at Bull Run, losing their colonel, James Cameron, brother of the secretary of war in Lincoln's cabinet, and several of their best officers. Later in the war, when they lost heavily in a desperate charge, the Charleston *Mercury* said, "Thank God, Lincoln has, or had, only one Seventy-ninth Regiment."

Scandinavians were scattered through almost all the regiments from Minnesota and Michigan. Company C, 27th Michigan Infantry, is a good example of how thoroughly immigrants mixed into the Union army. It contained twenty-two Canadians, sixteen Irishmen, thirty-eight Germans, twenty Englishmen, two Frenchmen, one Swiss, three Scotchmen, and one Welshman, in addition to fifty-five native-born Americans. One officer tells of having fifteen nationalities in his regiment, which required him to issue commands in seven languages.

Like the Irish, most of these men were motivated by a deep affection for their adopted country, which, often for the first time in their lives, offered them equal justice under the law. Here is how a Norwegian immigrant described his decision to enlist:

When I saw the danger in which our dear Union stood, I believed that it would not be right for me to lay my hands in my lap but must do what I could to be helpful to defend the laws which should assure our lives and our property. I turned first, after I had consulted with God about my duty, to my wife; she was at first not willing to let me go; then after further consideration she felt that perhaps it might be her duty to let me go, since there was a call from the authorities for help and God's word teaches that we should be obedient to them. . . . Our families stood praying as we left those who are our second selves and with moved hearts we took our departure.

A statistical study shows that one in every five Union soldiers was an immigrant—more than 500,000 out of the 2,312,304 Union enlistments. Two groups which enlisted in especially large numbers deserve to be mentioned. No less than 53,352 Canadians and 54,508 immigrants from England joined the Union cause.

Equally important in the ranks of the Union army, especially

Company E, 4th U.S. Colored Infantry in the Civil War. From *Photographs of the War of the Rebellion.*

during the closing years of the Civil War, were Negro soldiers. Some 186,000 fought to free their black brothers still in slavery behind the southern lines. They served in the artillery, in the cavalry, in the infantry, and in the engineers. At first, they had to endure the discrimination of lower pay. But after many protests, the War Department, beginning in 1864, paid Negroes as much as whites. When Grant besieged Lee before Richmond in the climactic struggle of the war, some thirty-four Negro regiments were in his army.

But the largest of all the immigrant groups in the Union army were the Germans. This was even more remarkable when we consider that there were not as many Germans as Irish in the United States when the war began. The explanation lies in their enthusiasm for Abraham Lincoln. It was not Lincoln, the emancipator, they admired, but Lincoln, the politician, who rejected the Know-Nothing influence within the Republican Party, and resolutely supported the voting rights of foreign-born naturalized citizens against Know-Nothing attacks. Without the votes of the German communities throughout the Midwest, Lincoln would never have become president. By regiments and companies, the Germans marched to support the president when the fighting started.

It was German courage that kept the state of Missouri in the Union. The governor was a Confederate sympathizer who openly wooed southerners in the state and encouraged them to arm and organize. The prize was the United States Arsenal in St. Louis, with its collection of 60,000 muskets, 1,500,000 cartridges, and machinery for turning out more guns. A West Pointer, Captain Nathaniel Lyon, was guarding the arsenal with a handful of Federal troops. When the Germans rallied to the Unionist cause, Lyon organized them into regiments and drilled them secretly.

The governor summoned his home guard and began drilling them on the outskirts of St. Louis for what was obviously to be an assault on the arsenal. Lyon boldly marched his Germans out to the southern camp, surrounded it, and disarmed the seven hundred would-be rebel soldiers. As they marched back to the armory, the German regiments were attacked by pro-southern St. Louis civilians, and a fierce street fight erupted, in which twenty-eight men were killed and many more wounded. The pro-southerners were temporarily routed, and, thanks almost entirely to the loyalty of the German regiments, the Federal government retained control of St. Louis and Missouri remained in the Union.

As more and more Germans swarmed to the colors, they were organized into regiments. The Federal government decided to let them fight under their own officers whenever possible. The command of the XIth Corps of the Army of the Potomac was given to General Franz Sigel. Fifteen of the twenty-six regiments were listed as German. Throughout the entire army, Germans were so proud of Sigel's rank that they told everyone they met, "I fights mit Sigel."

The Irish had no trouble communicating with their fellow Americans. But the Germans had the problem of a language barrier. Many of their enlisted soldiers, and not a few of their officers, could speak no English. Inevitably, this tended to make some Americans treat them in a rather contemptuous way. At the battle of Chancellorsville, this language gap almost led to disaster. German officers of the XIth Corps repeatedly warned the Union high command that the Confederates were planning an attack. The reports were brushed off. Then out of the woods poured twenty-five thousand southern veterans, the cream of Robert E. Lee's army, to smash the ten thousand men of the XIth Corps. After fighting against this steamroller for the better

General Franz Sigel.

part of an hour, seeing position after position overrun, the survivors fled in disorder toward the rear. The rest of the Union army was soon reeling back in an equally disordered retreat. After the battle, some Union generals blamed the Germans for the disaster. This was worse than unfair. If they had heeded the warnings of Sigel's men, the army would never have been surprised in the first place.

Determined to regain their good name, the Germans fought hard and well in subsequent battles. At Chattanooga they proved their courage and their loyalty for all time. Attacking Confederates on Lookout Mountain in what was to be called the "battle above the clouds," their orders were simply to "demonstrate" against this seemingly impregnable southern position. But the German soldiers scrambled up the almost perpendicular slopes under heavy artillery fire, and made a final bayonet charge up a two-hundred-foot incline strewn with boulders. They swept over the Confederate rifle pits on the crest of the mountain and threw the enemy into headlong retreat. Thanks to the victory, the Union army under General William Sherman was ready to begin the march through Georgia to the sea. This great thrust into the heart of the south all but ended the war.

After Sigel, the most famous German soldier was Carl Schurz. As a young man he had fought for freedom in Germany and had been driven out by Prussian tyranny. He was, like most Germans, a burning foe of slavery. Although he was only thirty-three years old, Lincoln sent him to Europe as envoy to Spain. He was soon warning the President that European opinion would turn against the North unless Lincoln transformed the war into a crusade to emancipate the Negroes. He finally persuaded Lincoln to let him come home, and Lincoln asked him to help in solving the emancipation problem.

On March 6, 1862, Schurz gave a speech at the Cooper

Carl Schurz.

Union in New York advocating emancipation. "Would rebellion have broken out if slavery had not existed?" he cried. "Did the rebellion raise its head in any place where slavery did not exist?" The speech was well received and it encouraged Lincoln to issue the Emancipation Proclamation a few months later. Schurz then persuaded the President, as a reward, to let him enter the army, where he served with distinction, first as a brigadier general and later as a major general.

In 1864, Schurz returned to Washington, D.C., to campaign for Lincoln's re-election. It was a summer of terrible discontent. Grant's losses in Virginia were staggering, and many northerners were calling on Lincoln to abandon his candidacy. Schurz played a key role in reassuring Lincoln that "the people, undisturbed by the bickerings of his critics, believed in him."

When the war was over, Schurz urged a policy of moderation on his fellow Republicans. "The best revenge for the past," he insisted, "is that which furnishes us the best assurance for the future." But the native Americans who controlled the Republican party after Lincoln's death did not listen to him. Schurz's fellow immigrants, satisfied to have proven their loyalty to America and defeated for good the Know-Nothing assault on their rights, did not respond to his idealism. On the contrary, his fellow Germans began pursuing even more energetically a dream which had obsessed them from the beginning—a new Germany in America.

5

DEUTSCHLAND IN AMERICA

GERMANS HAD COME to America in a steady stream since 1830. There were about 700,000 of them in the United States by the time the Civil War started. But this number did not approach the enormous influx of the post-Civil War decades. An additional 787,468 had arrived by 1870, and in the next two decades 2,144,438 flocked to *das land der umbegrenzten möglichkeiten* (the land of unlimited possibilities), putting the Germans far ahead of all other non-English nationalities. Today, experts estimate that one in six Americans can trace all or part of his ancestry to them.

To these Germans was handed the challenge of thrashing out one of the fundamental choices made by millions of immigrants who came after them: whether to accept the American culture or to try to preserve their own traditions. At first they veered alarmingly toward a "stockade" mentality. Their sheer numbers made it easy to do. The fact that they usually came in solid family groups, often with substantial financial resources, meant that their memories of the mother country were not nearly as bitter as those of the Irish. They were, by and large, far better educated, and they had already acquired an intense pride in German *kultur.* Germany itself was just beginning to achieve true nationhood in the post-Civil War decades, and her universities, her music, her art, her writers were blossoming under the impact of this new national pride.

Leaders such as Carl Schurz urged the Germans to give up their clannishness and stop living in segregated districts. Milwaukee, sometimes described as the "Munich of the West," suffered, in Schurz's opinion, from the presence of too many Germans. He urged his fellow Germans not to forget that "we as Germans are not called upon here to form a separate nationality but rather to contribute to the American nationality the strongest there is in us."

But the Germans declined to heed this advice. They were too content with the intensely German world they had transported with them to America. Central to every German community were the gymnasiums, or *turnvereins,* which organized young Germans into "Turner Societies." Almost as common was the German academy, where the children studied exclusively German texts and spoke almost no English. They were taught by German schoolmasters, who tended to look with contempt on Americans who attended public schools.

For older Germans an equally important social center was the *bierstube,* where they spent their Sundays drinking quantities of their favorite brew. In the *bierstubes* and at home, the Germans celebrated their traditional holidays—*Fasching,* the festival that precedes Lent; the celebrations just after Easter, when bock beer was in season; the *sommernachtfests,* when steins of beer were lifted in the parks and outdoor beer gardens.

Most elaborate of all the year's celebrations was Christmas.

The Turn-Halle in Milwaukee, 1864.

A group of Turners posed with athletic equipment, around 1880.

A group of girl Turners with Indian clubs, 1885.

Before the Germans arrived, the Anglo-Saxons and the Irish
had tended to celebrate this annual feast with whiskey-drinking
and fist-fighting. The Germans made it a family occasion,
contributing the custom of the Christmas tree, the blazing Yule
log, and many kinds of delicious cookies, as well as the jovial
figure of Santa Claus. (He was originally Dutch but was
heartily accepted by Germans as well.)

Herman Hagedorn, the biographer of Theodore Roosevelt
and others, recalled in his memoirs how his family celebrated
Christmas. He particularly remembered the *honigkuchen.*
"Those golden brown cookies were an essential part of the show.
You couldn't imagine Christmas without them. Mother made
them by the barrel and though she gave them away generously,
we generally had some well into February." The *veinnachstube*
was a separate Christmas room, sealed off from the children
until Christmas Eve. "The suspense of that final hour before
the giving of gifts, the *bescherung!*" Hagedorn recalled
fondly. His father would line up the family, and they would
all march upstairs to the Christmas room singing "Silent Night"
and "O Tannenbaum."

All this was part of what the Germans called *gemütlichkeit*—
a jovial enjoyment of the best things in life. Often this attitude
clashed sharply with the puritanical tendencies of native Americans. An especially sore point were the so-called Blue Laws,
strictly enforced in hundreds of American communities, forbidding all sorts of activities on Sunday. A primary plank in the
Know-Nothing platform was closing down the Irish saloons and
the German *bierstubes* on Sunday—an attack that aroused the
usually stolid Germans to a wrath that almost equaled the
Irishmen's more flammable temper. This hostility from the native Americans only inclined the Germans to build even higher
the walls of their stockade mentality. The post-Civil War years,

This satiric and exaggerated cartoon, "A German beer garden in New York City on Sunday Evening," reflects the unsympathetic attitude of many Americans toward the social activities of the newly arrived German immigrant. From *Harper's Weekly,* October 15, 1859.

with the enormous influx of their fellow countrymen, strengthened the trend. But the Germans soon found themselves in violent conflict with their Irish fellow immigrants.

A heavy percentage of the second wave of Germans were Catholics, fleeing the Prussian Protestant influence that was settling its iron hand over all of Germany. In America they found to their considerable astonishment that the Catholic Church was completely dominated by the Irish. As one observer of the scene wrote: "The Germans are a pillar of the Church in America but the Irish have always held the rooftop." The trouble began in the Midwest, where the Germans far outnumbered the Irish. Many Irish priests began warning bishops of a German plot to seize control of the Church as a major step toward creating "a young Germany" in the heartland of America.

There was considerable evidence for the charge. In some German-dominated religious orders, such as the Redemptorist Fathers, Irish and native-American seminarians had to learn German as a first step to becoming a member of the order. More and more German parishes put out signs saying, "German spoken here," and abandoned all but the most rudimentary interest in English. Meanwhile, resentments grew. German priests pointed out that of the sixty-nine American bishops in 1886, thirty-five were Irish, and only fifteen were German (and these included Swiss and Austrians). The Irish, remembering the Know-Nothing assault on "foreigners," became more and more alarmed at this German insistence on clinging to their native language.

Added to this was the temperamental clash between the two groups. To the German the Irishman seemed fickle and unstable. To the Irishman the German was dull and plodding. Moreover, not a few Irish bishops joined the native Americans in backing some kind of a law against the sale and use of liquor —what came to be called prohibition. Archbishop John Ireland

of St. Paul, Minnesota, often invaded tenements in his district
and flung whiskey bottles into the street. He did not care
whether they belonged to Germans or to Irish. Germans, with
whom drunkenness was not a problem, resented this interfer-
ence intensely.

The conflict came to a boil in August, 1883, when a German
layman named Peter Paul Cahnsley visited the United States. A
member of the German Reichstag and a wealthy philanthropist,
Cahnsley decided the Irish were persecuting the Germans. Back
in Europe, he began working subtly behind the scenes to influence powerful European churchmen. In 1891, a French priest
from Albany, New York, read a paper at a Catholic congress in
Belgium in which he claimed that out of the twenty-five million
Catholic immigrants who had entered the United States, twenty
million had lost the faith. This enabled Cahnsley to come forward with a proposal known as the Lucerne Memorial, after
the Swiss city in which it was drawn up. It suggested that the
Pope divide the United States into seventy-five territorial di-
visions with separate parishes for each nationality. A priest of
the same national origin was to be appointed to each parish.
Bishops would be appointed on the same principle. If the Germans were the majority in a diocese, the bishop would have to
be German.

The Irish regarded the controversy as crucial, not only for
the future of the Catholic Church in America, but also for the
status of every immigrant in American society. To encourage
immigrants to retain their native language would completely
reverse the Irish policy of urging all immigrants to learn English
and become American as quickly as possible. An even uglier
note was the report from Europe that Cahnsley had the secret
backing of European governments, who wanted to retain influence with their people in America.

James Cardinal Gibbons of Baltimore, the leading Catholic spokesman in America, condemned the Lucerne Memorial, and President Benjamin Harrison joined him. Thanks largely to Gibbons, the Pope ruled in favor of the Irish policy, although ethnic parishes were permitted for first-generation immigrants. It was a momentous decision for both the Church and America. If Cahnsley had won, other immigrant groups might have followed the German example and set up a series of permanent ethnic stockades which would have made the United States a nation of nations instead of a nation of nationalities.

But even if the Germans had built their *kultur* stockade, they would have found it difficult to maintain because they soon found themselves surrounded by new immigrants from other lands.

First to come were the Swedes—100,000 in the 1870's, 300,000 in the 1880's. Some Swedish villages lost half their inhabitants in a single year. No less than 1,250,492 eventually made the long voyage—a huge number for a country of barely 8,000,000. On their heels came the Norwegians, 846,000 strong, plus 355,301 Danes. If we count Norwegian immigration through 1915, it totals more than four-fifths of the entire population of Norway at the beginning of the nineteenth century. No other country except Ireland lost a larger proportion of her people to America.

Scandinavian immigration was inspired by a series of crop failures and economic crises in Sweden in the 1860's. Steamship companies and "America letters" from immigrants who had already ventured into the New World created the "America fever" which practically emptied whole villages. Land was what they wanted, and the great plains of the Midwest, the fertile valleys of Minnesota were like a magnet to them. By boat and covered wagon they poured into this promised land where a

This photograph of a dugout sod house in Oklahoma and the family that lived in it was taken around the turn of the century. Because of the lack of trees on the great plains, sod cut in long thick strips was the primary building material for many pioneers' homes. When a large portion of the house was built underground, there was less need for building materials, and the indoor temperature remained cooler. Photo by J. V. Dedrick of Taloga, Oklahoma.

Another form of sod house was built entirely above ground. This was the bachelor house of the Perry Brothers in Custer County, Nebraska, 1886.

160-acre homestead—twenty times the size of the average cotter's plot in Sweden—could be had for the asking.

Life on the prairie, in the early years, was harsh. The immigrants lived in sod huts and worked on railroads and canals for extra money to build decent houses. Hans Matson, a Swede who rose to prominence in Minnesota, later recalled the early years:

Looking back to those days, I see the little cabin, often with a sod roof, single room used for domestic purposes, sometimes crowded almost to suffocation by hospitable entertainments to newcomers; or the poor immigrant on the levee at Red Wing, just landed from a steamer in his short jacket and other outlandish costume, perhaps seated on a wooden box, with his wife and a large group of children around him, and wondering how he shall be able to raise enough means to get himself ten or twenty miles into the country, or regain the bedding or other household goods which he has perchance left in Milwaukee as a pledge for his railroad and steamboat ticket. . . . Poor, bewildered, ignorant, and odd looking, he had been an object of pity or derision all the way from Gothenburg or Christiania [in Sweden] to a little cabin of some countryman of his where he found rest and shelter until he could build one of his own.

Many Swedes were bitterly disappointed by what they found in these early days. Reality did not live up to the glowing descriptions of the steamship lines and the "America letters." One man wrote back, "We often find that he who relates that he owns a sawmill only owns a saw and sawbuck, and he who describes the beautiful carriage he owns, is the owner of a wheelbarrow for which he himself serves as the locomotive." Another man lamented that the home in which he first stayed was "much poorer than any charcoal hut in Sweden, without floor, almost without roof, and with a few stones in a corner which was supposed to be a stove."

But the land continued to beckon them with its potentialities. In 1853, Fredericka Bremer wrote of Minnesota: "What a glorious new Scandinavia might not Minnesota become! Here would the Swede find again his clear romantic lakes, the plains of Scandia rich in corn, and the vallies of Norrland; here would the Norwegian find his rapid rivers, his lofty mountains . . . and both nations their hunting fields and their fisheries. The Danes might here pasture their flocks and herds and lay out their farms on richer and less misty coasts than those of Denmark."

Perhaps the best description of Scandinavian life in the pioneer days is the novel *Giants in the Earth,* by the Norwegian immigrant Ole Rölvaag. His son, former Governor of Minnesota Karl F. Rölvaag, recently recalled his father's deep involvement with his immigrant past:

Dad was a man who was a completely integrated American, but also a strong believer that the best in America came from many national groups, many national origins and many racial backgrounds. He was a firm believer that the American culture was enriched by the contributions of men and women of all races, all colors, all creeds.

Because of this belief that the Norwegian and Scandinavian background had much to contribute to the American culture, he insisted that in our formative years (i.e. before we began school) we should speak Norwegian in the home. He knew full well that once we began the public school system English would be the spoken and written langu-

HARCOURT, BRACE & WORLD, INC.

Carl Sandburg, the son of an uneducated Swedish immigrant, was born in Galesburg, Illinois, in 1878. He drove a milk wagon at the age of thirteen, worked as a porter in a barbershop, stage hand in a theater, dishwasher, and harvest hand. He did not receive notice as an author until he was thirty-six, when his poem "Chicago" was published. He went on to become one of the best-known American poets, as well as one of the most respected biographers of Abraham Lincoln.

age, and he wanted us to be bilingual. Therefore, at home we always spoke Norwegian, though father was excellent in the usage of the English language, and one could scarcely detect that he had not come to this country until he was twenty years of age.

Another memory I have very clearly and indelibly in my mind of father occurred some time during the "Twenties" when the Ku Klux Klan had become rather active in Minnesota, mainly directed against the Catholics and particularly against the Irish Catholics. There was a rather prominent businessman in our community who had joined the Klan and had participated in some of its activities. This man was a member of our church, and I knew him and his son rather well.

After one outrage, and I don't remember the particular outrage at the time, my father said, "What a fool! Doesn't he realize that if we permit this to be turned against our Catholic brethren that next the venom will be turned against the Lutherans? He doesn't understand that he, too, is a "Johnny-come-lately" to America. Why shouldn't they be as violently against the Norwegians as against the Irish?"

Within this Scandinavian tide flooding into the Midwest came a smaller wave of 340,761 Dutch. Finally there came a little-known but significant second wave of English, who began abandoning the mother country in unprecedented numbers during the 1850's, when 394,237 came over. By the 1880's the figure had swelled to 810,900. These newcomers were soon pushing the Irish and the Germans hard for a place in the American sun. They were the last of what historians called "the old immigration." The diverse ways in which they entered the mainstream of American life is a dramatic story in itself.

❧6❧

MANY HANDS,
MANY DOORS

FOR THE IRISH, politics became the profession of opportunity in the last half of the nineteenth century. They organized potent political machines in New York, Boston, Albany, Chicago, and other major American cities where they clustered in large numbers. A political machine was organized like a pyramid, with a boss at the top of each ward, and each of the ward's districts headed by a lesser chief who got out the votes and took care of the people. The Irish did not invent the idea of voting in blocs. They learned it in Ireland, from English landlords, who marched their tenants to the polling places, where they voted under their master's vigilant eye.

New York boss George Washington Plunkitt described why and how the Irish were successful politicians:

What tells in holding your grip on your district is to go right down among the poor families and help them in the way they need help. I've got a regular system for this. If there's a fire on 9th, 10th or 11th Avenue any hour of the day or night, I'm usually there with some of my election district captains as soon as the fire engines. If the family is burned out, I don't ask whether they are Republican or Democrats and I don't refer them to the charity organization society which would investigate their case and in a month or two decide they were worthy of help about the time they are dead from starvation. I just . . . fix them up until they get things runnin' again. It's philanthropy, but it's politics too— mighty good politics. The consequence is the poor look up to George W. Plunkitt as a father, come to him in trouble— and don't forget him on election day.

With their mass of votes as bargaining power, the Irish were able to wangle thousands of their followers into the police and fire departments and into other city and state jobs. As early as 1855, they constituted a fourth of the 1,149 policemen in New York. In the growing city of Chicago, 49 of the 107 police on the force had Irish names. An O'Leary headed the police force in New Orleans, and Malachi Fallon was chief of police in San Francisco.

In New York the symbol of Irish power was the Tammany Society. Named after Chief Tammany, an imaginary Indian sachem, it was organized by native Americans in the last years of the eighteenth century as a part of the Democratic-Republican party of Thomas Jefferson. Their platform of fair play and justice for the poor and underprivileged naturally attracted the Irish immigrants, whose numbers soon overwhelmed Tammany and made it an all-Irish show. They quickly transformed Tammany into what one writer has called "an Irish village writ large." The hierarchy of party positions descended from the county leader to the block captains and even to building cap-

This cartoon of the Tammany Tiger, although undated, was obviously published at the time when the Irish influence in the society was strong. Note the hat and shamrock and the horseshoe tie clasp.

tains. Eventually the county committees of the five boroughs came to number more than thirty-two thousand persons.

They were a strange mixture, these Irish political machines, carefully controlled, yet full of rebellious characters, their leaders sober and industrious men—but always with a touch of Irish flamboyance. A startling percentage of the chiefs began their careers as prizefighters.

In 1875, one Tammany brave, ex-heavyweight champion of the world John Morrissey, called on Mayor William Wickham, whom he had helped to elect. One of Wickham's aides at City Hall asked Morrissey for his calling card. In a rage because he had no card, Morrisey stamped out. A few days later he marched through City Hall park dressed in a swallowtail coat, patent leather boots, and white kid gloves, with a light coat over his arm. A goggle-eyed friend asked him, "Hello, John, what's up now? Going to a wedding?"

"No," answered Morrissey, "not so bad as that, I just bought a French dictionary to help me talk to our dandy mayor. I'm going in full dress to make a call, for that is now the style at the Hotel Wickham."

The Irish, of course, loved him for it.

George Washington Plunkitt described the reaction of the top Tammany leaders to the news that they had just elected (in 1897) the first mayor of the consolidated city of New York. He told how a crowd followed the leaders across the street to a restaurant expecting a big celebration, with oceans of champagne. Instead, one leader ordered seltzer lemonade, another bicarbonate of soda, and another Vichy water. "Before midnight we were all in bed, and next mornin' we were up bright and early attendin' to business while other men were nursin' swelled heads," Plunkitt said.

These political machines operated as a kind of shadow government, and they had their own standards, their own ethics. A man's word was his bond. A leader never promised a favor unless he could deliver. A political job—or any other kind of job—was always given to the man who was "in line" for it. Loyalty to the organization was more important than obeying the law. Often this led to political corruption—bribe-taking for political favors and police "protection" of gambling and other

A CHOICE OF LEADERS

Kelly: Get out of this Ring, Morrissey. You know why we don't want you here.
Morrissey: Yes, I know—it's because I always "played a square game." But I'd like to see any swallow-tail put me out against my will. Besides, if you're backed by a few, I am backed by the many; and majorities rule.

This cartoon by J. Keppler satirizing a Civil War between Tammany chiefs appeared in *Frank Leslie's Monthly Magazine,* August 28, 1875. It is interesting to note that the cartoonist dressed the chiefs and braves in Indian garb. The society obviously retained its "Indian" image long after it was named after an imaginary Indian sachem.

illegal practices. But most of the Irish in politics were honest. The real power of the political machine lay in the enormous amount of money which the city and the state spent each year to build roads, canals, sewers, schools, hospitals, reservoirs. Here the Irish took care of their own, and Irishmen prospered in such businesses as construction, insurance, real estate, and hauling and carting.

At first glance the Irishman seemed unstable and highly emotional. But there was another side to his makeup—a deep peasant patience—and this made him an admirable candidate for the banking and financial worlds, where profits were small but gradually accumulated over the years to substantial amounts. Irishmen soon became prominent in financial circles. James V. Forrestal, the son of an immigrant, was president of the Wall Street investment firm Dillon Reed and Company before he entered politics and became America's first Secretary of Defense. The Emigrant Savings Bank was founded by Irish immigrants and remains today one of the largest savings banks in the nation, and still very much an Irish affair.

One study of distinguished American Catholics, the majority of them Irish, showed that 48.6 percent were lawyers or priests. A study of Catholic businessmen found 25 percent of them in finance, two-thirds more than the national proportion for other groups. Again the Irish account for this unusual imbalance. At the same time, they had a strong repugnance for trade. Only 7.7 percent of Catholic businessmen, barely a quarter of the national average, pursued trade as a career.

Joseph Kennedy, the son of an Irish saloonkeeper, sums up in himself and his family the major themes of the Irish in American society. Kennedy took the profits from his father's saloon and became a banker. His financial wizardry enabled him to make a fortune reorganizing companies, particularly in the movie business. His fortune made, he gravitated back into politics, and his sons followed him.

The Kennedys represented the idealistic side of Irish politics, but they were not an isolated phenomenon. Many Irishmen fought for clean government. Charles O'Conor, the lawyer who prosecuted Boss William Marcy Tweed—a native American who stole a hundred million dollars from the city of New York

A 1946 photograph of John F. Kennedy; his maternal grandfather, the former mayor of Boston, John (Honey Fitz) Fitzgerald; and Edward M. Kennedy, age fourteen. Shortly after this picture was taken, John F. Kennedy won his first political victory to become a Congressman from Massachusetts.

—was a second-generation Irishman. The reformer Lincoln Steffens, writing at the turn of the century, reported that Philadelphia, bossed by native Americans, was more corrupt than Irish-run New York. Thomas J. Walsh, a second-generation Irish Catholic, was the senator from Montana who exposed the Teapot Dome scandal in the 1920's.

Most famous of all, before the Kennedys cast their glow over the American political scene, was Alfred E. Smith, the "Happy Warrior" with the brown derby who was of Irish and German blood. Worshipped by the Irish of New York, he was the first Catholic to seek the White House. His 1928 campaign ended in failure, but he brought the Democratic party into power in numerous large cities around the nation, and prepared for the triumph of Franklin D. Roosevelt in 1932. At least as distinguished, if not as famous, was Frank Murphy of Detroit, who served as attorney general of the United States and later as a Supreme Court justice. In the words of one historian, Murphy was "one of the most valiant and forthright champions of the Bill of Rights ever to sit upon that high tribunal."

Meanwhile, other immigrant groups were playing different roles. In business and industry, German influence was enormous. John A. Roebling, a graduate of the Royal Polytechnicum of Berlin, invented wire rope and built the Brooklyn Bridge. Otto Mergenthaler, from Wurtenburg, revolutionized printing with the invention of the Linotype machine. George Westinghouse invented the air brake and made countless contributions to the field of electricity. Even greater was General Electric's genius, Charles P. Steinmetz. The Rockefellers in oil, the Schwabs and Fricks in steel, the Studebakers and Chryslers in automobiles—all came from German immigrant families.

Westinghouse was not only an inventor but, like most Ger-

MUSEUM OF THE CITY OF NEW YORK

Laying the cornerstone of the new building of the Tammany Society, January 8, 1929. Front row, left to right: Willis Holly, Secretary of the Society; Mayor James J. Walker; John R. Voorhis (one hundred years old), a Grand Sachem of the Society; and Alfred E. Smith, A Sachem of the Society, who had run for the Presidency of the United States in 1928.

mans, a shrewd businessman. He held onto his air-brake patents and formed his own company to manufacture them, as well as other railroad devices he invented. This poor farm boy, born in upstate New York to German parents, revolutionized railroading in America. He was a full-fledged industrial magnate by the time he was thirty. "Like a lion in the forest," his friend Nikola

John A. Roebling, inventor of wire rope and builder of the Brooklyn Bridge. From *Harper's Monthly,* May 1883.

Completed in 1883, this is how the Brooklyn Bridge looked from the Brooklyn side, around 1900. The glass slide, made by the Wittemann Brothers, from which this print was taken has been damaged over the years.

George Westinghouse, inventor of the air brake. From *Munsey's Magazine,* December, 1912.

John D. Rockefeller, Sr. This portrait of the oil magnate was painted by the famous American portrait artist, John Singer Sargent, in 1917.

Tesla said of him, "he breathed deep with delight the smoky air of his factories."

The German ability to organize large enterprises was ideally suited to the vastness of America. John Jacob Astor made millions developing the fur trade that opened up the Northwest. Henry Villard pushed the Northern Pacific through to the coast. Frederick Weyerhauser became America's lumber king. John D. Rockefeller amassed the greatest fortune in American history, by organizing the oil business. Walter Chrysler owed his preeminence in the automobile business not only to his mechanical genius, but to the skill with which he merged a half dozen small motor firms.

Side by side with this tycoon tendency was German activity in the labor movement. Some of the Germans were heavily influenced by the writings of Karl Marx, the father of communism, while others espoused the violent doctrines of the Russian anarchist Michael Bakunin, whom Marx expelled from the ranks of European communists. In 1886, someone threw a bomb into a squad of police in Chicago's Haymarket, killing seven policemen and four other persons, and injuring over a hundred others. The police had been on the scene to keep order at a demonstration held by an anarchist group to demand an eight-hour working day. The police arrested eight anarchist leaders for murder; six had German names. Although there was little evidence against them, their trial was conducted in an atmosphere of hysteria, and all were found guilty. Four were hanged, three received life sentences, and one committed suicide in jail.

Their philosophy was summed up by one of them shortly before he died. "Dynamite is the equilibrium, it is the disseminator of authority." A year later, another German immigrant, John Peter Altgeld, the governor of Illinois, pardoned the three men

A drawing of the Haymarket bombing by T. de Thulstrup from sketches and photographs furnished by H. Jeanneret. From *Harper's Weekly*, May 15, 1886.

who had been sent to prison for life. He had carefully reviewed the evidence and decided their conviction was unjust. The courageous act ruined Altgeld's promising political career. Many historians think that he might have become the first immigrant to reach the White House, if he had not pardoned the so-called Haymarket Bombers.

Partly because of the public outcry against the Haymarket violence, and partly because violence seemed out of place in a nation where change could be achieved by democratic methods, the anarchist movement lost its appeal to most Germans. But they remained heavily influenced by the ideas of Marxism— particularly the idea that the government should own and control the nation's industries. Thus they gravitated naturally into the Socialist Party, which believed in peaceful conquest through the ballot box. Victor Berger, editor of the German-language paper *Vorwärts,* was the first socialist to be elected to the U.S. Congress (in 1911) and for many years he was head of the Socialist Party in Milwaukee, the citadel of American socialism. By 1916, twenty-one of the twenty-five councilmen in the city were socialists, and so was the mayor.

The influence of socialism carried German-Americans out of the mainstream of the American labor movement, leaving the leadership of organized labor largely to the Irish. The Noble Order of the Knights of Labor, the first significant attempt to build a great national army of labor (in contrast to small craft unions) was led during most of its years of power—from 1879 to 1893—by Terence V. Powderly. Another Irish-American, Peter J. McGuire, is remembered as the father of Labor Day. He was also one of the founders of the American Federation of Labor, and served as its secretary and as a member of its executive committee for many years. Irish-American John Mitchell became president of the United Mine Workers of America in 1898.

The Scandinavians were not far behind the Germans in their contribution to America's wealth and power. With ax and saw—often called the Swedish fiddle—they cleared an estimated fifteen million acres of American soil, largely in the Midwest. Watching a gang of Swedish track layers pushing his Great Northern Railroad westward, tycoon James Hill exulted, "Just give me Swedes, snuff, and whiskey and I'll build a railroad through hell." Few other immigrant groups learned English as rapidly, or applied as eagerly for naturalization papers as the Swedes and their fellow Scandinavians from Norway and Denmark.

Scandinavians have been especially notable in their contributions to American science. The Stromberg carburetor in your car was invented by John Gullborg, its starter by Vincent Bendix, the disc clutch by George Borg. Your radio and TV sets contain at least twenty inventions by Ernst Alexanderson, the former chief engineer of General Electric. A Swedish sailor, Wilhelm Mattson, organized the Matson Navigation Company. John Ericsson, born in Stockholm, contributed not a little to the Union victory in the Civil War with his creation of the ironclad *Monitor,* which slugged it out with the Southern ironclad the *Merrimac,* and saved the wooden-hulled Union fleet from destruction. Ericsson also perfected the screw propeller and won a prize awarded by the American Mechanics Institute for a steam fire engine. Ole Evinrude, a Norwegian, invented the outboard motor in 1909, and became president of a corporation which for many years manufactured half of the nation's outboard motors.

Most immigrants became neither millionaires nor inventor-geniuses. It was the vastly expanding world of American sports that gave the newcomers their real heroes. For the Germans it may have been Honus Wagner, baseball's fabulous Flying Dutchman, or one of Yale's first all Americans, Bill Heffelfinger.

The Irish could choose between "Iron Man" McGinnity, who pitched forty-eight games in a single season, or Big Ed Delahanty, who won both the National and American League batting championships, or pint-sized John McGraw, star of Baltimore, later the hero-manager of the New York Giants. But in earlier, more primitive, days, neither baseball nor football led the sport scene. The prizefighter was the king—and immigrants of all nationalities found their superhero in John L. Sullivan.

The son of Ireland's shillelagh champion, the Boston strong boy acted out what every immigrant dreamed of doing—he put his fist in the face of life and knocked it down. He began at nineteen, mounting the stage of Boston's Dudley Street Opera House to challenge Tom Scannel, a well-known local fighter. In less than two minutes Sullivan clouted Scannel into the orchestra pit and then strode to the edge of the stage to deliver his mighty bass boast. "My name's John L. Sullivan and I can lick any man in the house. If any of 'em here doubts it, come on!"

Sullivan's title fight with Paddy Ryan, the "Troy Terror" and reigning champion, sent the entire country into a frenzy. Oscar Wilde, the famous English poet and dramatist then touring America, reported it for a British magazine. The Reverend Henry Ward Beecher, the best-known clergyman of the era, wrote a series of articles on it for another magazine. The fight lasted only seven rounds. "When Sullivan struck me," Ryan said, "I thought that a telegraph pole had been shoved against me endways." Sullivan went on to fight the last bare-knuckle defense of the heavyweight title against Jake Kilrain. It lasted two hours and sixteen minutes, or seventy-five rounds, and ended when Kilrain collapsed from exhaustion.

When Boston decided to pay formal tribute to its hero, the mayor and council had to rent a theater. John L. received a fifteen-minute ovation when he entered to accept a ten-thou-sand-dollar diamond and gold belt, four feet long and a foot wide. Nothing fazed Sullivan after that. On a triumphant tour of the British Isles, he spent two hours with the Prince of Wales, and on departing assured reporters, "Anyone can see he's a gentleman, the kind of man you'd like to introduce to your family."

John L's success lured Irishmen by the dozen into boxing. For thirty years they dominated the sport, and when men of other nationalities began to compete, they at first had to take Irish names, because the promoters were convinced that only an Irishman could draw the crowds. But compete they did, uneasily answering to their Gaelic monickers. A fiery little featherweight named Joe Carrora, winner of over a hundred bouts as Johnny Dundee, was among the first to signal that a new era was be-ginning in American immigration.

7

SONS
OF ITALY

ALTHOUGH ITALIANS did not come to the New World in any
great numbers until 1880, they could hardly be called strangers
to American shores. Hadn't the country been discovered by one
Italian and named after another? Moreover, there is scarcely a
history of the new continent that does not mention a pair of
Italian sailors—Giovanni da Verrazano, the man who first sailed
into New York Harbor (some fifty years before Henry Hudson)
and Giovanni Cabot—John Cabot—the Genoese pilot who, in
1497, discovered the mainland of North America.

We have already seen the important roles individual Italians,
such as Francisco Vigo and Phillip Mazzei, played in America
during the revolutionary decades. In the years that followed,
this tradition continued. Individual sons of Italy, many of them
gifted artists, musicians, and scholars, came to America, usually
as political refugees, and found a ready audience for their talents.

In 1805 President Thomas Jefferson recruited a group of Italian instrumentalists to form the Marine Corps band. The band still plays at White House receptions and similar official functions, and up until a few years ago the majority of its members still had Italian surnames. Jefferson also wrote to his old friend Phillip Mazzei, who had by then returned to his homeland, and asked him to enlist Italian sculptors and painters to help build the United States Capitol. Much of the stonework, murals, and statues in the building are the work of Italian immigrants. However, the most famous artist, the man who has been called the "Michelangelo of the U.S. Capitol," did not arrive until some years after Jefferson's death.

His name was Constantino Brumidi, and he made the decoration of the Capitol his life's work. "My one ambition," he wrote, ". . . is that I may live long enough to make beautiful the Capitol of the one country on earth in which there is liberty." So proud was Brumidi of his adopted land that he signed one of his paintings—a huge mural of the surrender at Yorktown that now hangs in the restaurant of the House of Representatives—*C. Brumidi, artist. Citizen of the U.S.*

Brumidi spent twenty-five years—from 1855 to 1880—in Washington. He did many of the other paintings in the Capitol, including the giant fresco inside its famous dome. At the age of seventy-two, he was still working on the frieze in the Capitol rotunda. One day, painting a series of panels with scenes from American history, the artist slipped from his scaffold. Luckily he managed to cling to the platform and hung there, some sixty feet above the stone floor, until rescuers came. Brumidi was uninjured but his doctors said that the shock contributed to his death a few months later. His pupil and fellow countryman Filippo Costaggini was commissioned by Congress to continue his work.

1)   2)

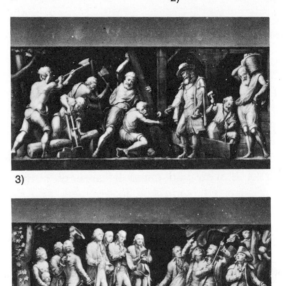

3)

4)

The four sections from the frieze in the Rotunda of the U.S. Capitol Building shown above are: 1) "Landing of the Pilgrims at Plymouth, Mass., 1620;" 2) "Penn's Treaty With the Indians, 1682," the section on which Constantino Brumidi was working when he slipped from the scaffold; 3) "Settlement of Plymouth Colony, 1620," the first section to be completed by Filippo Costaggini after the death of Brumidi; and 4) "Reading of the Declaration of Independence, 1776," also by Costaggini. A slight difference in style between the two artists can be seen, even though Costaggini was working from Brumidi's sketches. The entire frieze is eight feet high and extends 300 feet around the circular dome of the Capitol. Despite the sculptural appearance of the work, the entire frieze is painted in wall-flat fresco.

Another Italian who made an important contribution to American culture was Luigi Palma di Cesnola. Di Cesnola came to the United States in 1860, served as a brigadier in the Civil War, and earned a Congressional Medal of Honor for his valor. He won further distinction after the war as the U.S. consul in Cyprus. While there he became a pioneer in excavating the island's ancient ruins. In 1879, di Cesnola was named director of the newly organized Metropolitan Museum of Art. He is credited with building it into one of the foremost museums in the world.

In 1820, the first year the United States started keeping immigration statistics, only thirty Italians entered the country. Sixty-two came the following year, and even in 1833, one of the peak immigration years, the number of Italians was still less than two-hundred. The majority of these immigrants were educated people who had come because of political unrest in their homeland. They were scholars and language teachers, musicians and artists, highly educated, mostly from northern Italy. They were regarded with respect and welcomed in the very best circles.

1880, however, marked a radical change in Italian immigration. Up until then, a mere twelve thousand Italians had taken up permanent residence in the United States. After that date, some twelve thousand Italians were entering the country in a single day. Unlike their predecessors, they came from the poorest sections of southern Italy and had little or no education.

America, they had heard, was a land of plenty. Roads, pipelines, and reservoirs were under construction; new office buildings and factories were springing up in the cities. There was an urgent need for labor of all kinds at wages which, compared to a peasant's meager earnings, sounded like the income of a millionaire.

Italian immigrants who have just arrived at the Battery in New York. This photograph was taken around 1890 by H. A. Wise Wood.

The owners of America's factories were delighted to find a source of cheap manpower but the new immigrants were greeted with little enthusiasm by the rest of the country. Their swarthy skin and strange language made them suspect to begin with. Like the Irish before them, they were mostly uneducated farmers who took the most menial jobs they could find. Their wages were so low that they were forced to live in ugly, overcrowded tenements in still uglier and more overcrowded slums. A New York newspaper editorial expressed the sentiments of many "old" Americans when it declared in 1888, "The flood gates are open. The bars are down. . . . The sewer is unchoked. Europe is vomiting. In other words, the scum of immigration is being viscerated upon our shores."

The poor and illiterate immigrants became known as dagoes, wops, or guineas, and were the objects of physical as well as verbal attack. "You don't call an Italian a white man?" one Cali-

This drawing, entitled, "Plying the Old Trade in the New Country," appeared in *Harper's Weekly* in 1873. It is an example of one of the more subtle forms of class prejudice directed against Italians by America's older and more established immigrant groups.

fornia employer was asked. "No sir, an Italian is a dago," was the reply.

One tragic incident occurred in New Orleans in 1890. The chief of police was shot down under mysterious circumstances and died swearing that his attackers had been "dagoes." The chief had furnished no other description of the men, but on the basis of this statement, a mob of local citizens mustered on the docks to greet a shipload of Italian immigrants who had the bad luck to arrive in the port just at this time. They jeered and cursed at the new arrivals, leaving them totally confused but otherwise unharmed.

Eventually a group of Italians was seized and held for the police chief's murder. None were convicted but the judge nevertheless sent them all back to jail. A few days later, an angry mob stormed the jailhouse and, taking the law into their own hands, killed eleven of the prisoners, to the exultant shouts of the onlookers who had swarmed down to watch the lynchings.

The rest of the country was horrified at the New Orleans massacre. Ironically, the bloodshed brought to the city still another Italian immigrant. Her name was Frances Cabrini, and she was a Missionary Sister of the Sacred Heart. She and a group of other nuns set up a hospital, an orphanage, and a shelter for any immigrant in distress. She brought comfort not only to the families of the lynching victims but also to the entire Italian population of New Orleans. Later, she was to do the same thing in other cities in the country, and much later, in 1946, some thirty years after her death, she was named by the Roman Catholic Church Saint Frances Xavier Cabrini—the first citizen of the United States to be canonized.

Some of the most violent anti-Italian feeling was generated by the Sacco-Vanzetti case, which began with the robbery of a payroll for a Massachusetts shoe factory in 1920. The rumor

An officer escorts the handcuffed Bartolomeo Vanzetti (center) and Nicola Sacco (right).

quickly spread that the thieves had been Italian, and two immigrants, Nicola Sacco and Bartolomeo Vanzetti, were soon arrested. Their case was complicated by the fact that they were both outspoken anarchists, and at this point, just a few years after the Russian Revolution, the United States was experiencing a violent reaction against communists and anarchists, particularly when they were immigrants. In another trial dominated by public hysteria, Sacco and Vanzetti were found guilty. Both men were executed in 1927. Students of the case are still debating whether they were really guilty of the crime. One thing is certain: much of the evidence on which they were convicted was flimsy and irrelevant.

Many were quick to have Italians carted off to prison and to assume they were guilty despite the absence of any kind of evidence. This attitude was blatantly expressed in a magazine article that appeared about a year before the New Orleans massacre. "What have the dagoes to lose by pilfering, assaulting, robbing and murdering? As far as creature comforts are concerned, they live better and work about as much, have warm clothing and better beds, in the meanest jail in the United States than they experienced out of it."

Some of the Italians were disgusted with the New World. Used to toiling in vineyards and gardens, they found it impossible to adjust to cramped city living, and returned to Italy. Many more, however, decided to send back home for their families, and despite the poverty and congestion, the sneers and name-calling, stayed and became Americans.

It is hard to believe that life in the new country was better than it had been in the old. Jacob Riis, a reporter who was himself an immigrant from Denmark, told of one Italian family in which the twelve-year-old daughter went to school at night and spent most of her day making linen-covered pocket flasks. For this she earned about sixty cents; her mother, who took in sewing, made slightly less. The family lived in a dark, airless tenement facing out on a grimy alleyway.

"Of Susie's hundred little companions in the alley—playmates they could scarcely be called," Riis wrote, "some made artificial flowers, some paper-boxes, while the boys earned money at 'shinin'' or selling newspapers. The smaller girls 'minded the baby,' so leaving the mother free to work."

To add to their woes, the immigrants often suffered at the hands of their own people. They were exploited by contractors called *padrones* who imported young men and boys almost like indentured servants, The padrones, in exchange for paying their passage over and the promise of a job, kept the greater part of their wages. The padrones often acted as bankers for other immigrants and kept most of the money they were supposed to bank.

The Italians repeated the Irish experience of exhausting work

A New York newsboy. Many youngsters from immigrant families contributed to family incomes by going to work at an early age.

on railroad and construction projects. Here is how an eyewitness described one group of Italian railroad workers on the job:

> *. . . The rails were heavy and the men worked with might and main all the forenoon. There was no let-up, no mercy. From shortly after five until twelve, about seven hours, the men labored without rest. "The beasts," said the* padrone,

"must not be given a rest, otherwise they will step over me."
As the men silently appealed to him for mercy, I was filled
with pity, and often during the day attempted to beg the
padrone to let them rest. But how could I approach a raging
maniac? He was what the railroads wanted. . . . After seven
hours of the hardest labor the younger men had sausages
and bread; the older men were satisfied with bread alone.
Yet, with coffee in the morning and bread at noon, these
men worked for ten hours every day under the blistering sun
or in pouring rain. . . . Stopping work at four, the men
returned to their ramshackle cars to cook, eat, and sleep.

Under the pressure of such a harsh way of life, and battered
by the recurrent waves of prejudice and the degradations of the
slums, it is hardly surprising that some Italians turned to crime,
as the Irish had before them. Unfortunately, they brought with
them a ready-made organization that made crime a more tempt-
ing and lucrative way of life. It was called the Mafia, a name
given to a number of organized bands of Sicilian brigands in
the nineteenth and twentieth centuries. Its tradition went back
to feudal times, when nobles hired outlaws to guard their estates,
in exchange for protection from royal authority. Organized into
loosely linked groups called "families" headed by one mobster,
the Mafia rose to power in the United States during the 1920's,
when the nation attempted an ill-fated experiment in the prohibition of alcoholic beverages. By ruthlessly eliminating competi-
tors with bombs and bullets, the Mafia swiftly gained control of
much of the illegal, "bootleg" sale of liquor in many large cities,
and after prohibition was abandoned in 1933 they used their
profits to establish control of other "rackets," such as illegal
gambling, narcotics, and prostitution.
But the Mafia represents only a tiny percentage of Italian-

Americans. Most of them preferred to pursue America's opportunities honestly. Despite all the hardships and prejudice, the New World offered one thing that the Old World had lacked—hope. One young man, Rocco, writing about his experiences, told of living in a room with five other immigrants, rising at 5:30 in the morning to go to work, and for his dinner buying meat that was cheap because it was so old and tough nobody else wanted it. Rocco and one of his friends started out shining shoes, but business was so good that they soon were able to open their own shoeshine parlor and had enough money left over from their earnings to go to the theater and take their girl friends to Coney Island. "We were very ignorant when we came here," nineteen-year-old Rocco wrote home to his family, "but now we have learned much."

While many immigrants, by dint of hard work and careful savings, managed to open their own restaurants, shoemaking shops or barbershops, few rose quite so spectacularly as Amadeo Pietro Giannini. Giannini's father, an emigrant from Genoa, had been a padrone of an Italian colony in San Francisco. Amadeo expanded his father's operations and become a bona fide banker. His Bank of Italy came to the rescue of many Italians whose homes and businesses were leveled in the famous San Francisco earthquake of 1906. Soon after the holocaust, Giannini was out on the streets with a wagon full of cash. Depositors could withdraw their savings on the spot; those who wanted a loan could watch as Giannini dipped into the two million dollars he had brought along and doled out the amounts. Often only a man's honest face or his callused hands served as security.

The young banker's investment in the rebuilding of his city eventually paid off handsomely. His Bank of Italy grew into the Bank of America, one of the largest and most prosperous financial institutions in the world.

A)

BANK OF AMERICA

B)

BANK OF AMERICA

C)

BANK OF AMERICA

A) Amadeo Pietro Giannini was the son of a Genoese immigrant and the founder of the Bank of Italy in 1904. B) The first Bank of Italy was housed in this building at the corner of Washington Street and Columbus Avenue in San Francisco. C) The modern World Headquarters Building of the Bank of America in San Francisco. Today, only sixty-six years after its founding as the Bank of Italy, the Bank of America is the world's largest commercial bank.

Another highly successful immigrant was Generoso Pope. He started his career as a waterboy for a construction gang and worked his way up to become the owner of one of the country's largest sand and gravel businesses. He also became publisher of the Italian-American paper *Il Progresso*. One of the first things he did after he became a millionaire was to donate an electric light plant to the tiny Italian village of Arapaise, where he had been born.

A young writer named William Seabrook visited Generoso Pope in his office one day in 1938 and asked him about the rumors that he could afford butlers and footmen and a staff of servants as big as Mrs. Astor's. "Do you really want to know why I have so many?" Pope said. "My wife had to do all the cooking and washing when we were poor. She worked as hard as I did, never complained, has stuck to me through thick and thin, has borne me fine children . . . and now I want her to have everything, everything she can have."

Pope was often honored by Italian-Americans and was treated like a celebrity back in Italy, but he once said: "The happiest I've ever been is the moment I became a full-fledged American citizen. America has done everything for me."

While names like Giannini and Pope were well known in the business community, other Italian immigrants and their sons were achieving fame in other ways. One of the most outstanding of these was Fiorello LaGuardia. The son of an Italian bandmaster in the U.S. army, LaGuardia was born in New York but spent much of his youth in Europe. A short, burly, fast-talking politician, he will be remembered as one of New York City's best and liveliest mayors. In addition to dashing off to fires and reading the funnies over the radio to the city's children, LaGuardia also occasionally took advantage of his right as mayor to preside in court.

Fiorello LaGuardia in 1938.

Once during the height of the Great Depression an old man was brought before him charged with stealing a single loaf of bread. He needed the food, he said, because his family was starving. LaGuardia felt that he had to fine the man. So he did. But he reached into his own pocket and took out ten dollars to pay the fine. Then he promptly remitted the penalty and tossed the bill into the wide-brimmed hat that was his trademark. "And furthermore I hereby fine every person in this room fifty cents apiece, except the prisoner, for living in a town where a man has to steal in order to eat." The old man walked out of the police court with $47.50 and, as one reporter phrased it, "the light of Heaven in his eyes."

Perhaps the most triumphant story of Italian immigration is the career of Edward Corsi. He was born in the ancient village of Capestrano in Italy. His father died and his mother remarried and came to America with his stepfather, a brother, and two sisters. They had heard that it was a wonderful place and that they would all soon be rich. Corsi remembered standing on the foredeck as their boat steamed up through the Narrows and into New York Bay. Mothers and fathers held up babies, children surged against the rail, all looking at the Statue of Liberty.

Edward stared at what he thought were mountains and pointed them out to his brother Giuseppe. "If they're mountains," Giuseppe demanded, "why don't they have snow on them?" The mountains, it turned out, were the skyscrapers of lower Manhattan. The Corsis passed through Ellis Island, the twenty-seven-acre way station in New York harbor which served as the gateway to America for millions of immigrants between 1892 and 1943. The family settled on the Lower East Side in what Corsi later described as "four sordid tenement rooms." There was, he recalled, "but one outside window and this looked down on a dingy street." As soon as he was old

COMMUNITY SERVICE SOCIETY

In this photograph, taken about 1920 for the Mulberry Health Center in New York City, a nutritionist is instructing a group of women in a tenement home on the Lower East Side.

enough, Edward had to go out to work. His first job was as a lamplighter, and he had to get up at four in the morning to put out the lamps on his route. A succession of similar odd jobs as a messenger or clerk enabled him to pay his way through Fordham University. He then became director of a settlement house where he himself had played as a boy. He worked to make life easier for the new immigrants who still poured into the area. There were playgrounds for the children, classes in English and citizenship, social clubs for the parents.

In 1931, Corsi received a singular honor. President Herbert Hoover appointed him commissioner of immigration at Ellis Island. He was the first immigrant to hold the post. When he was appointed, one of his friends congratulated him and remarked to him that he now had one of the most important jobs in the country.

"You'll be helping to *make* America," the friend said. "After all, you know, this nation is only sixty-five percent Plymouth Rock. The other thirty-five percent is Ellis Island."

"I know," Corsi replied quietly, "I'm part of that thirty-five percent myself."

In the decades since 1880, the sons and daughters of Italy have, by and large, moved out of their slums and tenements and up from their jobs as ditchdiggers and day laborers. They have gained fame in widely assorted careers. Show business can claim—among others—Frank Sinatra, Dean Martin, and Jimmy Durante. Politics has been a ripe field for Italian immigrants. They have taken over as mayors of several dozen cities. Foster Furcolo and John Volpe have served as governors of Massachusetts, Michael DiSalle as governor of Ohio. Equally distinguished is John A. Pastore of Rhode Island, the son of an immigrant tailor who not only served as governor of his native state but also had the honor of being the first American of

An Italian feast day in New York. From *Harper's Weekly*, April 1881. Similar festivals are still held every year in New York's Italian neighborhoods. The Feast of San Gennaro on Mulberry and Prince Streets is perhaps the most popular.

Italian descent to be elected to the United States Senate. On September 12, 1968, Francis John Mugavero, son of Sicilian immigrants, became bishop of Brooklyn, the biggest Catholic diocese in America.

But many Italian immigrants who have become neither rich nor prominent have nevertheless displayed a remarkable depth of feeling for the land that was discovered by their countrymen. Some years ago a factory worker named Frank Rusto who lived in the small town of Vicksburg, Michigan, was left a great deal of property. All he had to do to claim it was renounce his American citizenship and move back to Italy. Rusto took one look at the letter that suggested he move back to Italy and shook his head. "That I will not do," he replied, "I would rather be a papermill worker in Vicksburg than the king of Italy."

8

THE
CHOSEN PEOPLE

"SUSPENDERS, COLLAH BUTTON, 'lastic, matches, hankeches—
please, lady, buy." In the 1880's the traditional cry of the Jewish
peddler could be heard up and down the streets of New York.
He was a greenhorn—a newcomer—but he had heard and seen
how others prospered in the land of opportunity. With hard
work and a little luck, perhaps he too would someday be rich.

It was not an impossible dream. One of the most successful
men in the city, Joseph Seligman, lived in a splendid house on
fashionable Murray Hill. A Jew from Germany, Seligman was
now a banker, but as an immigrant he had started his career
trudging through the small towns of central Pennsylvania with a
pack full of shawls, ribbons, buttons, and thread slung over his
back.

The itinerant merchant was not new in America. In the
earliest days of the country, most of them had been from
Connecticut or Massachusetts—the famous Yankee peddlers.
In the mid-nineteenth century, their numbers dwindled; ped-

Banker, Joseph Seligman.

MRS. EDITH LAFRANCIS

This typical peddler's wagon belonged to William Mayer of Hartford, Connecticut; and his sign advertises brooms, agate ware and tinware in exchange for old clothes.

dling was a hard, lonely, and often dangerous life. But like other immigrants before them, the Jews were in no position to be particular about job status or working conditions. They eagerly replaced the Yankee peddlers, and more than a few used their profits to launch themselves as manufacturers, bankers, and department store owners.

We have already seen the way individual Jews, or small groups such as the Sephardim (the Spanish and Portuguese Jews), became part of the American nation during the colonial and revolutionary years. Until the middle of the nineteenth century, the number of Jews in America was small—probably somewhere between one and two thousand. They were treated with respect possibly because they were so few. In many places they were regarded as curiosities. When Joseph Jonas, a watchmaker, became the first Jew to settle in Cincinnati, in 1817, people came from all over the countryside to look at him. An old Quakeress said to him: "Art thou a Jew? Thou art one of God's chosen people. Wilt thou let me examine thee?" After making him turn around several times, the lady finally sniffed and declared, "Well, thou are not different to other people."

Soon after the beginning of the nineteenth century, Jews began coming to the United States in larger numbers. Most of them came from Germany to escape the various wars and persecutions that took place after Napoleon's defeat in 1815. The refugees were poor, ragged, and uneducated. The Sephardim, most of whom were among the successful businessmen, turned up their noses at the new class of Jewish immigrants. In their fashionable houses and secure businesses, they wanted nothing to do with the tattered, ill-spoken foreigners who seemed to find no work but peddling.

The new breed of Jewish immigrants, however, quickly graduated from shopkeeping and peddling and into their own banking and brokerage firms. By the 1860's and 1870's families like the Lehmans, Loebs, Guggenheims, and Seligmans were among the wealthiest in the country. They owned splendid mansions along Fifth Avenue and summer "cottages" in the Adirondacks and along the Jersey shore, and they traveled to Europe in style.

One notable success story was that of Lazarus Strauss, who came to the United States in 1854 with his three sons, Isidor, Nathan, and Oscar. The family started a small crockery and glassware business and in 1896 were successful enough to buy R. H. Macy's in New York, which under their ownership developed into the world's largest and most famous department store. Isidor served in Congress and was twice offered the nomination for mayor of New York. Oscar served as U.S. minister to Turkey and was secretary of commerce and labor under President Theodore Roosevelt. Nathan, a pioneer in public health, set aside part of his vast fortune to organize milk stations where milk could be sold cheaply or distributed free to those who could not afford it.

Some Jewish traders went as far afield as California. There is a plaque in San Francisco commemorating the High Holiday services conducted by forty Jewish pioneers in a room above a store on September 26, 1849. One of the most famous of the western merchants was Levi Strauss, a Bavarian who headed west from New York around 1850 with a stock of canvas that

Levi Strauss.

LEVI STRAUSS & CO.

The factory of Levi Strauss & Company in San Francisco as it appeared in 1880.

he planned to sell for wagon covers and tents. The cowboys and miners he met along the way complained that they could not find pants sturdy enough for their work, so Strauss cut up the canvas and stretched it into tight-fitting pants. At his customers' suggestions, he riveted the pockets on with copper nails so their tools would not rip them off. The result was the formation of Levi Strauss & Co., and the discovery of the jeans, or Levis, that are today one of the most popular items of clothing in the country.

Most of the German and Sephardic Jews were solidly established in the United States when the third—and by far the
largest—wave of Jews arrived. Around this time, Emma Lazarus, a descendant of Sephardic Jews, wrote a famous poem to
help raise funds to bring the Statue of Liberty from France.
Christening the statue "Mother of Exiles," she put stirring
words on Liberty's "silent lips."

> *". . . Give me your tired, your poor*
> *Your huddled masses yearning to*
> *breathe free*
> *The wretched refuse of your teeming*
> *shore*
> *Send these, the homeless, tempest*
> *tost to me*
> *I lift my lamp beside the golden door!"*

Noble as these sentiments were, they contained some pain-
fully accurate descriptions of the new Jewish immigrants. This
third wave came from Eastern Europe—Poland, Rumania,
Lithuania, and Russia. They were fleeing from the cruelty of
the Czars, who forced them to live in segregated areas called
the Pale of Settlement. They were restricted from pursuing an
education or entering the professions. The Czar's soldiers frequently rode through the Pale evicting them from their homes,
and seizing their goods. Persecutions were commonplace, and a
pogrom, or massacre, could be decreed whenever it suited the
people in power.

It was not difficult to understand why a Jew would be
tempted to emigrate. Moreover, by 1870, many of the shipping
companies were no longer bringing Irish and German immi-

An engraving of Emma Lazarus by T. Johnson from a photograph by W. Kurtz, 1888.

The Statue of Liberty at dusk. Emma Lazarus' poem, "The New Colossus," written in 1883, appears on the pedestal at the base of the statue.

A Russian Jewish immigrant at Ellis Island, 1910.

grants to the New World, and they began seeking the business of the poorer people who lived farther to the east. Their business was helped by a cholera epidemic in 1868, a famine the year after, and the Odessa pogrom in 1871. The exodus began.

Forty thousand Russian Jews arrived in the United States in the 1870's. In the next decade, some 200,000 came; the next ten years brought 300,000. From 1900 to 1914, 1.5 million more arrived. Many of them were the wives and children of the earlier arrivals. Several thousand were Jews who had been dragged off to serve the Czar's armies in the Russo-Japanese War of 1904 but instead deserted across the nearest frontier and booked passage for America.

The wave of East European Jews that entered the country from 1880 to 1914 totaled almost two million. Many of them would eventually move on to Chicago, Detroit, or Philadelphia, but by far the largest percentage remained in New York and made their home on the city's Lower East Side. Living conditions were hardly better than they had been in Europe. Relatives and friends crowded into three or four small tenement rooms, most of which lacked windows, toilet facilities, or running water.

Fires were common, and most of the tenements were without fire escapes. Those who had them often found them so burdened with worn-out furniture or household possessions that they were completely useless. Some Jews' strict adherence to the laws of their religion spared them from many diseases of tenement life. They were always careful to cook their food properly and were compelled by their religion to practice personal cleanliness and to have their houses cleaned thoroughly at least once a week. Many, however, abandoned the strict demands of their faith under the harrowing stresses of slum life.

The new immigrants were subjected to abuse and derision, as almost every newcomer had been. A young girl from Poland recalled that the first words she heard on reaching her adopted homeland were a nasty chant:

> *Green Horn, Pop corn, five cents a piece,*
> *July, July go to Hell and Die.*

This was mild, of course, compared to the shouts of "Sheeny" or "Christ-killer" that were often hurled at the Jewish immigrants. What their tormentors probably did not realize was that these insults, although not pleasant, were nothing compared to the bloodbaths and persecutions of the old country. The Jews tried to close their ears and found consolation in the dreams of a better world that their hard work would create for their children.

The poverty and the miserable living conditions in the Jewish slums of the Lower East Side were almost as bad as the conditions the Irish had endured in their earlier immigration. Lillian Wald, who founded the Henry Street Settlement House, with its visiting nurse service, kept notes on her work. Here is an account of a visit she made in the area on July 2, 1895:

Climbing the stairs in search of Mrs. Schwartz (the mother of a child with ophthalmia, an eye disease) found terrible filth everywhere. Stairs filled with slops, floors reeking. I went into every room in the front and rear tenement, set the dwellers to sweeping, cleaning and burning refuse.
In some rooms swill thrown on floor, vessels standing in rooms unemptied from night's use.
I saw the housekeeper who promised cooperation in keeping the place cleaner.

Hutchins Hapgood, one of the first to study the life of the Jewish ghetto, wrote in 1902 about the agony of the newly arrived Jewish immigrant, confronted by an alien land and an alien language: "His deeply rooted habits and the worry of 'daily bread' make him but a little sensitive to the conditions of his new home. His imagination lives in the Old Country and he gets his consolation in the old religion. He picks up only about a hundred English words and phrases, which he pronounces in his own way."

On July 30, 1895, an anonymous contributor to the *New York Times* said of the Jews of the Lower East Side:

A writer might go on for a week reciting the abominations of these people and still have much to tell. One of their greatest faults is that they have an utter disregard for law. There is a certain hour when they are required to set out their garbage and ashcans, but they pay no attention to that. . . . Filthy persons in clothing reeking with vermin are seen on every side.

Many of these people are afflicted with diseases of the skin. Children are covered with sores and hundreds of them are nearly blind with sore eyes. . . . Cleanliness is an unknown quantity to these people. They cannot be lifted to a higher plane because they do not want to be.

Yet, almost miraculously, the atmosphere did not destroy the immigrants' spirit of creativity. In his biography, *Let There Be Sculpture,* Sir Jacob Epstein, the sculptor who won fame in Britain, recalled his life on the East Side during the 1880's. "This Hester Street and its surrounding streets were the most densely populated of any city on earth; on looking back at it, I realize what I owe to its unique and overcrowded humanity. Its swarms of Russians, Poles, Italians, Greeks, and Chinese lived as much in the streets as in the crowded tenements; and the sights, sounds, and smells had the vividness and sharp impact of an oriental city."

Earning a living was the overwhelming problem for the newcomers. Fortunately they were used to hard work and long hours. Many became peddlers. Others found work as cigarmakers, tailors, milliners, furriers, and dressmakers. Some became locksmiths, jewelers, and printers. Many more did a thriving business selling matzos, seltzer water, bagels, herring, and other popular foods to their own people.

THE BYRON COLLECTION, MUSEUM OF THE CITY OF NEW YORK

The Lower East Side of New York City (Orchard Street) as it looked in 1898. Photographed by Byron.

Whatever business they entered, they preferred to work for and with Jews, who understood their language and who would make allowances for their religious rituals, including the keeping of the Sabbath. Their wages were low. Many men earned only fifty cents a day. Yet from this small sum they would spend only ten cents for bagels and tea and try to save something, dreaming of the day when they would have enough money to bring their wives and children to America too. When they arrived, the wives and older children went out to work, at the same low wages.

Jewish children learned to take advantage of every free cultural attraction New York could offer: concerts in the park, parades and celebrations, and above all the libraries. One little girl who spent many happy hours in the library recalled the "quiet and the enormous rooms—living rooms were then an unknown quantity among our people."

Books were an avenue of escape from the grubby tenements. They were also a source of education. In Europe a professional education had been denied to most of the immigrants because of their faith. In America, they were no longer barred from such pursuits and no amount of sacrifice was considered too much to get a professional degree. Many would-be doctors clerked in shops or did piecework in factories while studying to enter medical school. Pushcart peddlers' sons became dentists, pharmacists, or lawyers.

But the climb out of ghetto living was not easy. For many years the immigrants worked in small factories, or "sweatshops," as they were commonly called. Conditions were unbelievably bad. Several dozen men and women would be crowded into a loft, hunched over sewing machines from early morning till late at night, with only a few minutes to grab a bite to eat or stand up and stretch their cramped muscles. Worst of all, many of the factories were little more than hovels, lacking toilet facilities, light, fresh air, and the most rudimentary of safety precautions.

The miserable plight of the factory workers was brought home to the entire country in 1911. A flash fire tore through the Triangle Waist factory just off Washington Square. Most of the workers were young women, and when the blaze was finally put out firemen counted 146 dead, dozens more burned or disfigured. Most of the dead had been trapped inside the flaming building but many had fought their way to the windows and leaped to the pavement below. The disaster was a heavy blow to the residents of the Lower East Side. Almost every family had a daughter, sister, or neighbor who had been killed or injured in the tragedy.

The investigation of the Triangle Waist Company fire pointed to such miserable working conditions that in 1913 a series of labor laws was enacted that considerably improved the lot of factory workers.

It is hardly surprising that Jews, who were so often the victims of unfair labor practices, should be among the leaders of labor reform. Samuel Gompers, a Jew from England who started

Samuel Gompers at the age of fifty.

NEW YORK PUBLIC LIBRARY

work as a cigarmaker at the age of ten, became one of the founders of the American Federation of Labor and was its president for almost forty years.

The German Jews at first scorned their more recently arrived brethren. It was in fact the Germans who coined the word *kike* because so many of the new Russian- and Polish-born immigrants had surnames that ended in *ki*. Nevertheless, the Germans felt an obligation to these people simply because they shared the same religion. Their contributions succeeded in establishing such organizations as the Young Men's Hebrew Association, the Educational Alliance, and the Hebrew Free School. They were designed to keep alive Hebrew history and religion and to teach the immigrants the "privileges and duties of American citizenship." Hospitals like Beth Israel and Mount Sinai were founded in the ghettos and originally treated only Jews. Today they are among New York's leading hospitals, and their patients come from all over the country and from every religious denomination.

The Russian Jews were determined to climb out of their ghetto as successfully as the Germans before them had done. An amusing story that exemplified the spirit of the Russian immigrants was once told by David Sarnoff, a multimillionaire who became a brigadier general in the United States Army and chairman of RCA—the Radio Corporation of America.

Sarnoff came from Russia with his parents in 1900. He was nine years old at the time and could not speak a word of English. His mother quickly enrolled him at the Educational Alliance for a course in English. He had been there a week and had made not a great deal of progress when his teacher gave him an assignment. He was to stand up at assembly and recite, "Cleanliness is next to godliness."

Young David studied the small speech until he knew it per-

General David Sarnoff, former Honorary Chairman of RCA. This picture by Karsh, Ottawa, was taken in 1961.

fectly. His schoolmates broadcast the event around the neighborhood and his parents and most of the neighbors showed up at the assembly. When Sarnoff heard his name called out, he rose and went up to the platform. But as he stood there gazing out at the sea of faces, he could not remember a single word of his carefully memorized speech. The teacher escorted him from the platform and he hung his head in shame at the family dinner table that evening.

The very next day, however, he decided to remedy the problem. He joined the debating society at the Educational Alliance and learned not only to speak English but to speak it with authority and hold his own in an argument.

Many years later, the Educational Alliance was celebrating its fiftieth anniversary. The mayor of New York and a host of other distinguished guests were at the celebration. General Sarnoff was invited to be one of the speakers. He briefly recalled the story of his failure and then said, "I have only one speech to make and I am going to make it right now: 'Cleanliness is next to godliness.' "

The Jews have distinguished themselves in almost every field of American life. No other group in the so-called "new" waves of immigrants have equaled their percentage of college graduates, or the income level they have achieved. Louis Brandeis, Arthur Goldberg, and Felix Frankfurter have sat on the U.S. Supreme Court. Jonas Salk, discoverer of polio vaccine, and Bela Schick, conqueror of diphtheria, are among the giants of modern medicine. Writers such as Saul Bellow and Bernard Malamud appear regularly on the best-seller lists. Show business abounds in Jewish names, only in sports have Jews been under-represented, in comparison to other immigrants. They have produced

Arthur J. Goldberg resigned from his position on the United States Supreme Court to become the United States representative at the United Nations. Here he is addressing the Security Council, May 24, 1967.

UNITED NATIONS

UNITED STATES

Dr. Jonas Salk, discoverer of polio vaccine.

some outstanding athletes, such as football star Sid Luckman, home-run slugger Hank Greenberg, and strike-out pitcher Sandy Koufax. But long centuries of cramped ghetto life in Europe made it difficult to create an athletic tradition.

The ghetto on New York's Lower East Side still exists. Hester and Delancy Street shops are still closed on Saturday sabbath and do a thriving business on Sundays. There are still poor people in the tenements, but few are Jewish. Most of the original inhabitants and their children have moved on to the suburbs, or to other sections of town, upward on both the social and economic scale.

Unfortunately, Jews still meet discrimination in many places. Some communities refuse to let them into their country clubs, or try to bar them from owning property, or confine them to certain streets or sections of town. It is not true everywhere, but it is shameful that it is true anywhere. America, the land of equality and opportunity, has offered the Jews opportunity, but some Americans still refuse to offer them equality.

❧9❧

FROM EAST
AND WEST

IN A SMALL, DESERTED CHURCH in Jamestown, Virginia, three persons stood before the altar. One held a book and recited the wedding ceremony in a low, gentle voice. The other two were a pretty, delicate girl and a big, husky young man. Their hands were joined, and they kissed each other when the man with the book said, "I declare you man and wife."

Julian Kulski, recently arrived in America, was reaching back into the immigrant past of his people to reestablish his roots. The marriage required the permission of the Secretary of the Interior and the cooperation of a priest. The young couple were turned down by two priests, but a third, struck by the originality of the idea, agreed to join them in the experiment. Why was Kulski going to all this trouble? He was the descendant of a 1610 Polish immigrant to Jamestown who had worshipped in this same church.

Thus did one young Polish newcomer take advantage of Poland's long participation in America's history. But after the first settlers at Jamestown, and the soldiers such as Kosciusko and Pulaski who fought for America's freedom during the Revolution, Polish immigration was only a trickle, compared to the masses from Ireland, Germany, and the other nations whose peoples came in great waves to the New World. Then, in the last decades of the nineteenth century and the first decades of the twentieth century, the Poles started their own "wave." Two hundred and thirty-six thousand entered the United States between 1890 and 1900, and this jumped to 875,000 between 1900 and 1910, cresting the year before World War I, 1912–13, when 174,365 entered in a single twelve-month period. By 1920, there were 3,000,000 Americans of Polish birth or parentage in the United States.

Most of these newcomers poured into the cities, where "Little Polands" soon blossomed. By 1920, Chicago had a Polish colony of 350,000, New York 250,000, Buffalo 80,000, Milwaukee 75,000, and Pittsburgh 200,000. Detroit, with the growth of the automobile industry, attracted 300,000 by 1930. Like the immigrants who preceded them, the Poles took the hard, exhausting jobs. But a surprising number of them—almost 750,000—soon turned to farming, and moved into areas in Massachusetts and the Connecticut valley abandoned by New Englanders. Edna Ferber's story *American Beauty* (1931) tells the story of reclaiming these abandoned farms, with deep admiration for the Polish appetite for hard work.

Although most Poles came as single individuals (men outnumbered women by about two to one) and were mostly refugees from the brutal poverty of peasant farming, they brought with them an intense devotion to their native land and six-hundred-year-old culture. In the first decade of the century, the Polish National Alliance, an active, forward-looking youth movement, organized special schools where second generation

Polish-Americans could study the language of their homeland on weekends. "The well-trained instructors often varied the two hours of study with folk songs and stories for the children who willingly forfeited a part of their weekend vacations to learn their mother tongue," proudly wrote one Polish commentator. The Polish National Alliance has about 340,000 members, publishes a newspaper, and has done much to maintain Polish consciousness among Polish-Americans, down to the present day.

In the beginning, of course, the Poles had to battle the same kind of prejudice that the Italians, the Irish, the Dutch, and other immigrants experienced. *Polack* became a term of contempt, and the Poles were lumped with other so-called "steerage slime from Eastern and Southern Europe." Prophets of doom predicted they would never become Americans.

The strange tongues and different customs of the southern and eastern European seemed, to the superficial observer, to support this argument. By 1903, when Emma Lazarus' poem was inscribed on a tablet and placed on the pedestal of the Statue of Liberty, the reaction against them was in full swing. The National Board of Trade, forerunner of the United States Chamber of Commerce, had come out for protection against "the scourgings of foreign disease, pauperism and crime." They were reflecting the views of the Immigrant Restriction League, organized in Boston by descendants of earlier English immigrants, who now considered themselves American aristocrats.

In the 1890's, thanks to their lobbying, Congress for the first time had passed a literacy test for adult immigrants. President Grover Cleveland promptly vetoed it, declaring that literacy was a test only of a person's past education and not of his future ability or worth as a citizen. When the Immigrant Restriction League lobbied to reintroduce the bill at the next session of

A)

A) This 1880 cartoon by J. Keppler, entitled "Welcome to All," expressed the feeling of most American immigrants. The United States was portrayed as an "Ark of Refuge" from the conditions in Europe at that time. Keppler, himself an immigrant, executed this cartoon with heart-warming gusto for the British publication *Puck.* B) Just eleven years later (1891) another cartoonist did this drawing for *Judge.* Captioned, "If immigration were properly restricted, you would no longer be troubled with Anarchy, Socialism, the Mafia and kindred evils," it reflects the sentiment of many Americans who favored restricted immigration.

B)

Congress, the immigrants of earlier years swung into action. They created an Immigration Protective League and fought hard against the bill. Officers of 150 German societies, for instance, issued a furious blast against it as a revival of Know-Nothingism.

Perhaps the best answer to the attack on the new immigrants came from Finley Peter Dunne, the son of Irish immigrants, who wrote an immensely popular newspaper column under the name of "Mr. Dooley." Dunne used his Irish wit to ridicule the pretensions of those who called for a halt to immigration: "As a pilgrim father that missed th' first boat, I must raise me claryon voice again' th' invasion iv this fair land be th' paupers an' arnychists iv effete Europe. Ye bet I must—because I'm here first. . . ."

Dunne proposed a meeting of "the Plymouth Rock Assocya- tion to discuss th' immygration question," which was to be attended by "Schwartzmeister an' Mulcahey an' Ignacio Sbar- baro an' Nels Larsen an' Petrus Gooldvink" and was to gather "at Fanneilnoviski Hall at th' corner iv Sheridan and Sigel sthreets." When his old friend Hennessy asked what was to be done with "th' offscourin' iv Europe," Mr. Dooley's reply was: "I'd scour thim some more."

Other Americans stoutly defended the new immigrants with facts. One of the most influential was Peter Roberts, who pub- lished a remarkable book about them in 1912. Roberts told of visiting a group of Poles who were working in a foundry in Rockland County, New York. The employers treated them well, gave them good salaries, took an interest in their living conditions. They gave prizes to the families with the best gar- dens. Only a few miles away there was a similar plant, where other Poles worked for dreadful pay and under awful living conditions. This plant had all sorts of trouble with its workers. When Roberts compared the peaceful atmosphere in the first plant, an executive told him: "Yes, but that company has a better group of Poles than we have—these men are no good."

Roberts' answer was to insist that there were no such things as bad Poles or good Poles, any more than Italians, Greeks, or Swedes were bad. All the new immigrants wanted was a decent life, and anyone who treated them fairly and honestly would find them first-class citizens. In fact, the country could not get along without them. Between 1880 and 1905 money invested in manufacturing plants had increased five times. Roberts told of asking a man who ran a tanning factory if he preferred to employ "foreigners."

"No," was the man's answer, "but the Irish and the Germans are gone and if this plant's to run, Italians, Lithuanians, and Poles must do the work."

In defense of these so-called "new" immigrants, who included not only Poles and Italians, but Hungarians, Greeks, Ukrainians, Czechs, and Slovaks, Roberts quoted the extensive investigation of the U.S. Immigration Commission. These experts declared: "The present movement is not recruited in the main from the lowest . . . strata of the population. . . . It represents the stronger and better element of the particular class from which it is drawn." This was a very important fact about immigration, which too many people ignored. It was easy enough to appreciate the courage of the Pilgrims and the earlier settlers who crossed the seas in tiny sailing ships. But the more recent immigrants, sailing on more modern ships, and spared the immediate danger of drowning, or of confronting a hostile wilderness, have been slandered as failures who could not "make it" in their own countries and fled to America. Actually, to leave the familiar world one has known from birth, and venture into a strange land whether it is civilized or a wilderness, requires great courage. Thus, it is only common sense, which scientific investi-

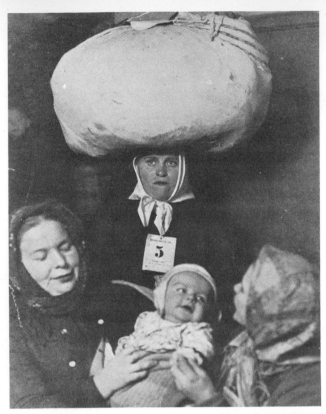

Slovakian immigrants at
Ellis Island in 1905.

A Hungarian group in national costume in Milwaukee, 1920.

gation has confirmed, that the superior people—those more intelligent, healthier, more vigorous—were the ones who accepted the challenge of America.

It also makes it easier to understand why the Poles, Italians, and other non-English-speaking immigrants tended to cling together inside their stockade mentality at first.

One of the problems created by the Poles' attachment to their own culture can be seen in this touching letter, published in a newspaper in 1913:

I am polish man. I want be american citizen—and took here first paper in 12 June. But my friends are polish people— I must live with them—I work in the shoes-shop with polish people—I stay all the time with them—at home—in the shop—anywhere.

I want live with american people, but I do not know anybody of american. I go 4 times to teacher and must pay $2 weekly. I wanted take board in english house, but I could not, for I earn only $5 or $6 in a week, and when I pay teacher $2, I have only $4—$3—and now english board house is too dear for me. Better job to get is very hard for me, because I do not speak well english and I cannot understand what they say to me. The teacher teach me—but when I come home—I must speak polish and in the shop also. In this way I can live in your country many years—like my friends—and never speak—write well english—and never be good american citizen. I know here many persons, they live here 10 or more years, and they are not citizens, they don't speak well english, they don't know geography and history of this country, they don't know constitution of America—nothing. I don't like be like them I wanted they help me in english—they could not—because they knew

nothing. I want go from them away. But where? Not in the
country, because I want go in the city, free evening schools
and learn. I'm looking for help. If somebody could give me
another job between american people, help me live with
them—it would be very, very good for me. Perhaps you have
somebody here he could help me?
If you can help me, I please you.
I wrote this letter by myself and I know no good—but I hope
you will understand what I mean.

> *Excuse me,*
>
> F. N.

"I wasn't educated and didn't know the language, so everyone took advantage of me and paid me in pennies," an elderly Polish worker recalled. "But each of my four sons has graduated from college."

This has been typical of the Polish approach to American life. They have scrimped and saved to give their children America's opportunities. They have also demonstrated a very Polish preoccupation with land. To own his own land was the height of glory and success for the Polish peasant in the Old World. The immigrants put aside a few dollars a week from their hard-earned salaries to achieve that dream in America. Soon Poles were buying their own homes in unprecedented numbers. Today more than four out of five of Chicago's Polish-American families own the homes they live in. Hamtramck, Michigan, the most solidly Polish city in America, is also noted for its high ratio of homeowners. In Bayonne, New Jersey, Polish-Americans for many years owned 60 percent of all the real property.

Like other immigrants, Poles have sought recognition on the playing fields. Although they compose only 3 percent of America's population, they have produced more than twice that percentage of major league baseball players. As early as 1916, Harry Kobelskie was the American League's pitching champion. And in the twenties there was Al Simmons, one of the greatest hitters in baseball's history. The apex of Polish baseball prowess was reached in the person of the genial St. Louis Cardinal slugger Stan Musial, who retired with a host of hitting records beneath his name, and was recently elected to baseball's Hall of Fame.

Poles have demonstrated a remarkable aptitude for science. Dr. Gerald Pawlicki has served as head of the Argonne National Laboratory, and Dr. Bruno J. Zwolinski is another physicist active in the National Science Foundation.

In politics, the Poles at first progressed slowly because of the language barrier, but this has long since vanished. No better proof of their acceptance—and prominence—as a significant part of American life has been the rise of Edmund S. Muskie, who achieved the unprecedented feat of getting himself elected

Senator Edmund Muskie of Maine.

governor and then senator on the Democratic ticket in once solidly Republican Maine. In 1968, Muskie ran for Vice President on the Democratic ticket.

While the Poles settled in the eastern and central parts of the United States, seldom getting beyond Chicago in significant numbers, another group of immigrants were treading a more painful path on the opposite side of continental America. The first Chinese came to America in 1820, but he did not exactly start a wave. By 1853, only eighty-eight had followed him. China was still very much a cloistered kingdom, cut off from the outside world. But the discovery of gold in California, and the westward rush of population that followed the news, drastically altered this pattern. Steamships were soon plying back and forth between San Francisco and Chinese ports, and on their return trips they invariably carried some Chinese immigrants. They were highly valued as general laborers, carpenters, and cooks. Because women were scarce, they quickly acquired a monopoly on the laundry business. They did the work that white men, busy looking for gold, considered either too hard or too unrewarding. By 1852, some fourteen thousand Chinese had become a part of the population of the new state of California. They eagerly participated in the customs of their new country. Some two thousand marched in a Fourth of July celebration in Placerville, California.

At the same time, like other immigrants, they clung to their inherited religions and customs. In San Francisco, they built a temple at an estimated cost of twenty thousand dollars—a huge sum in those days—and brought from China an idol valued at thirty thousand dollars. As California grew, thousands more Chinese came to work in the mines, or to build the great transcontinental railroads then being planned and constructed. In 1868, the United States signed a treaty with China permitting unrestricted immigration. But it specifically refused these immigrants the right to become citizens, as other immigrants did, by going through the process of naturalization. By 1869, over nine thousand Chinese were working for the Central Pacific Railroad.

Already they were experiencing, in a particularly cruel form, the prejudice which every immigrant has faced. They met it from the moment they landed in San Francisco. One eyewitness told of a typical hoodlum attack:

These Chinamen, with their shaven crowns and braided cues, their flowing sleeves, their peculiar trousers, their discordant language and their utter helplessness, seemed to offer a special attraction for the practice of those peculiar amenities of life for which a San Francisco hoodlum is notorious. They follow the Chinaman through the streets, howling and screaming after him to frighten him. They catch hold of his cue, and pull him from the wagon. They throw brickbats and missiles at him and so, often, these poor heathens . . . reach their quarter of this Christian city covered with wounds and bruises and blood.

As more and more Chinese arrived to work on the railroad, some compassionate white citizens of San Francisco formed a Chinese Protective Society and met each immigrant ship with special police to guard the bewildered arrivals.

An Irishman, working on the railroad, summed up the laboring man's antagonism when he complained that he and the other whites got thirty-five dollars a month and board. He considered this "coolie" wages, and blamed it on the Chinese, who were willing to work for such low pay. With a bitter look at the nearest Chinese, he added, "If it wasn't for them damned

This cartoon from *Frank Leslie's Monthly Magazine,* November 1877, shows the fear of the American workingman that his wages would be undermined by Chinese laborers, who were willing to work for less money.

nagurs we could get fifty dollars and not do half the work."

Soon the idea that Chinese labor was undermining the American standard of living became almost an obsession with the American workingman. Newspapers eager to raise their circulation did not help matters when they published largely fictitious stories about filth and immorality of various cities' Chinatowns and of the supposed violence of Chinese secret societies. Unfortunately, some unscrupulous American employers did use Chinese to intimidate American workers. In 1870, for example, Chinese were shipped from California to North Adams, Massachusetts, to replace striking shoemakers. When the American economy sagged into a depression in 1876, labor leaders and demagogues formed anti-Chinese societies and called on the country to repel the "Yellow Peril."

All-out rioting soon exploded in several cities. Twenty-five Chinese laundries were burned by gangs of hoodlums in San Francisco in the summer of 1877. At Rock Springs, Wyoming, twenty-eight Chinese were killed and fifteen injured in another riot. Earlier, fifteen had been hanged and six shot to death by rioters in Los Angeles. Ironically, the Irish, who had been the target of the Know-Nothings in the East, took the lead in attacking Chinese immigrants in California. One of the leaders was Dennis Kearney, whose slogan was, "Four dollars a day and roast beef."

"The Chinese must go" became the war cry of Kearney's Workingman's Party. Soon these hotheads were calling for revolution, to drive out not only the Chinese but the entire capitalist class. The party soon withered away, but not before it had frightened the Democrats and the Republicans into passing all kinds of restrictive laws against the Chinese in California and other western states. In 1880 both major parties backed the restriction of Chinese immigration in their national platforms.

A wood engraving after a sketch by H. A. Rogers, which appeared in *Frank Leslie's Illustrated Newspaper,* March 20, 1880, showing a meeting of the Workingman's Party on the sand-lots in San Francisco.

Soon a new treaty was signed with China, in which the Chinese government agreed to prevent further emigration to the United States—and haughtily insisted that this meant Americans would henceforth be excluded from China.

Many Chinese went home, disheartened by the prejudice they encountered in America. But thousands more retreated into their Chinatowns and pursued a quiet, inoffensive way of life. The census of 1920 reported 61,639 Chinese in the United States, with a quarter of them in California. By 1960, this total had grown to 237,292; most of these had been born here and were American citizens. Chinatown is a thriving tourist attraction in both San Francisco and New York, and thousands of Chinese earn their livings running restaurants in both these cities, preparing the exotic and incredibly varied foods of their homeland for American palates.

Dong Kingman teaching his class at the Famous Artists School. He was born in Oakland, California, and studied in Hong Kong. His art has been exhibited internationally, and in 1954 he made a cultural exchange lecture tour for the United States Department of State.

World War II brought many Chinese out of their isolation. They became stenographers, timekeepers, welders, carpenters, and shipyard and aircraft workers. One study of them reported, "As the younger Chinese moved out and went into the American community, antique shops, chop suey restaurants, and hand laundries began to close their doors." Another expert wrote, "One thing is certain, they have found a freedom they will not willingly relinquish." This has proved to be the case. A recent study of the Chinese family, done by the Community Service Society of New York, shows the younger generation moving out of Chinatown, marrying non-Chinese, and deliberately abandoning the traditional customs and ways of thought.

While the Chinese were retreating under the assaults of western Know-Nothings, another group of men with yellow skins were coming to America for the first time in significant numbers. One hundred and fifty-three Japanese came to Hawaii, under the sponsorship of an American businessman, in 1868. But not

STUART SMITH PHOTO, I. M. PEI & PARTNERS

Ieoh Ming Pei is well known as an American architect. He was born in Canton, China, and became a naturalized U.S. citizen in 1954. He is a member of the New York City Urban Design Council and has also been involved in redevelopment planning projects for several other major U.S. cities.

The Everson Museum of Art in Syracuse, New York, is one of the outstanding buildings designed by I. M. Pei. He also designed the National Center for Atmospheric Research in Boulder, Colorado; The John Fitzgerald Kennedy Library in Cambridge, Massachusetts; and the National Airlines Terminal at Kennedy International Airport in New York.

I. M. PEI & PARTNERS

Text on sign: CHINESE YOUTH for MAYOR · LINDSAY 請選林西市長

This photograph, taken at the time of New York's 1969 mayoralty election, reflects the new activism and involvement of the young Chinese American.

PUBLIC HEALTH SERVICE

Most Oriental immigrants to America arrived in San Francisco rather than in New York. Here a boatload of new arrivals is being inspected by medical officers of the United States Public Health Service, San Francisco Quarantine Station.

until 1885 did more follow. The Japanese government had a morbid fear that emigration would weaken the state, and only when the pressure of population made it clear they could not support their crowded millions did they permit more people to leave.

For the next twenty years, Hawaiian planters did everything but welcome Japanese immigrant ships at the Honolulu docks with brass bands. The island was desperately short of laborers, and by 1900, sixty-one thousand Japanese were in Hawaii, where they comprised more than 40 percent of the population. At the same time, ships blown off course or prevented by sickness aboard from landing in Hawaii occasionally deposited their human cargoes in California. Other Japanese, unhappy with Hawaii's limited opportunities, decided there was more hope for advancement on the mainland, and came voluntarily.

By 1900, there were about sixteen thousand Japanese along the American West Coast, most of them in California. They soon excited the same brainless prejudice which the Chinese had aroused. Hoodlums and bullies attacked them in the street and burned their restaurants. Newspapers once more trumpeted phony stories about the "Yellow Peril." But the Japanese continued to arrive in a fairly substantial wave, fifty-eight thousand from 1901 to 1910.

In 1906, the San Francisco city government, under investigation for massive corruption, tried to divert public attention by abruptly announcing that henceforth all Japanese pupils in the public school system were barred, and would have to attend a special segregated school. There were only ninety-three Japanese in San Francisco's twenty-three schools at the time, and twenty-five of them had been born in the United States. The Japanese government was outraged and protested strongly. In Tokyo, militarists who were even then arguing that Japan would have to fight a war with America and the other Western powers for their place in the sun were able to say, "See I told you so, these whites hate us." Theodore Roosevelt, the President of the United States, tried to have the law declared unconstitutional. He failed and was forced to negotiate with Eugene E. Schmitz, the crooked mayor of San Francisco, already under indictment. Finally, to get the law withdrawn, the President promised to reach "a gentleman's agreement" with the Japanese government to prevent further emigration.

Part of the agreement permitted Japanese already in the United States to bring in wives. Since nine out of ten of them were young, unmarried men, and lacked the money for the long passage home to find a bride, they arranged with relatives in Japan for so-called "picture brides," who were married to them by proxy in their home country, and then sailed to America to meet their husbands, for the first time. This trend, plus a trickle of Japanese entering illegally from Canada, Mexico, and Hawaii, added steadily to their numbers in the United States.

Most of them worked on California's huge fruit and vegetable farms, where their skill in handling delicate crops and their physical endurance at the hot, back-breaking work made them valuable employees. But like other Americans who came before them, the Japanese were determined to make America their land of opportunity. They saved their money and bought farms of their own, often in places which Americans either had abandoned or considered too swampy or dry to grow crops profitably. With patience and energy, the Japanese amazed their American neighbors by succeeding where white men had failed.

One Japanese spent ten years draining land along the Sacramento River delta, and finally turned it into the most profitable potato farm in the state. Another Japanese, in the Imperial Valley, discovered that lettuce grew beautifully on arid land that Americans had ignored. Others learned to control sandy, shifting soil by growing grapes and melons in alternating rows. By 1912, Japanese owned 331 farms, comprising 12,726 acres, and were leasing other farms, amounting to 137,000 acres.

This was, of course, a tiny part of California's twenty-eight million acres of farmland. But the big California farmers saw that if the trend continued, they would soon lose all their precious Japanese labor. So once more, they raised the cry of the Yellow Peril, and the California State Legislature enacted a bill forbidding "aliens ineligible for citizenship" from owning land. This applied only to the Japanese and Chinese. Oregon, Washington, and other western states soon passed similar laws, making it impossible for any immigrant Japanese farmer to be anything but a hired hand.

Thousands of Japanese, discouraged by such cruel and obvious prejudice, gave up and returned to Japan. But thousands more fought back as other immigrants had before them. They put the land in the names of their children who had been born in this country and who were therefore automatically American citizens. They found white Americans who agreed that the law was detestable and bought land in their names.

Not all the Japanese became farmers. Typical was Masaharu Ono, who worked first as a railroad section hand, and then opened a small shop in Los Angeles, stocking it with hardware and Japanese goods, wooden sandals, chopsticks, and other things that Japanese farmers might want to buy. He chose a picture bride and raised three children, two of them boys. He himself had come to America hoping to enter college and return to Japan as a scientist. He had never made enough money to realize this dream, but his children went to college. He made sure of that. Some years later, a study found that 46 percent of all the Nisei, (as Japanese born in the United States were called), between sixteen and twenty-four were in colleges or professional schools. They got better marks in schools than their white classmates. A Seattle high school reported that Nisei made up only one-tenth of the student body, but that one-third of the names on the honor roll were Japanese.

In Seattle, the Japanese took over a bleak section, full of old, dilapidated buildings which no one else wanted. They built up a tightly knit community, in which most of the members were small shop owners, or butlers or maids in private homes. They were intensely proud of their reputation, and always made it a point to subscribe fully to every civic project. Crime was practically nonexistent, while it was rampant in the surrounding slums. When a commission made a report on local crime, there was a white spot in the center of Seattle surrounded by black—a law-abiding island in a sea of lawlessness. The white dot was the Japanese section. One man said Seattle was white where it ought to have been black because it was yellow.

In San Francisco, Los Angeles, Stockton, Fresno, and other West Coast cities, the same pattern developed. To protect themselves from the prevailing hostility, the Japanese withdrew into these small, self-sufficient "little Tokyos" and lived out their quiet, hardworking lives. They had their own newspapers, and they sent their children to special after-hours language schools, as the Poles and, earlier, the Germans had. The stockade mentality became very strong. Prejudiced Americans used it to accuse the Japanese of being an exclusive, proud, unassimilable race. It wasn't true, of course. The "little Tokyos" were caused by the Yellow Peril mentality, which had blocked the first Japanese attempts to achieve equality.

Gradually, here and there, the stereotype of the Japanese as tricky, arrogant, bucktoothed thieves broke down. One writer tells of a white country family that was horrified when Japanese bought a neighboring farm. For months neither family exchanged a word, not even so much as a nod, with any member of the other family. Then, the white mother began noticing how clean and attractive the Japanese children were as they trudged home from school. She invited them in for a snack. Another day, watching the Japanese working late in the fields, she sent some cool drinks over to them. The Japanese responded by inviting her to dinner. Suddenly, the two families were friends.

Other white Californians began to realize they were the victims of their politicians, rabble-rousing labor leaders, and self-interested big farmers, who had trained them to hate an innocent people. H. A. Millis, in a careful and impartial report prepared in 1914, declared that the Japanese, far from being vicious and depraved, were known for their "efficiency, ambition, long employment and trustworthiness." In his book *Americans from Japan,* Bradford Smith tells of a woman raised in California who told him: "You know, I just realized the other day that all my life I've been taught to hate the Japs and never realized there was anything wrong with it. . . . I've grown up hating them. I didn't even know it was prejudice at all. I didn't know. And I always prided myself on being a liberal. How can people be like that? How can I?"

10

THE
ALMOST-CLOSED
DOOR

IN SPITE OF EFFORTS by many Americans to fight slanders and hostile myths about the immigrants, many racists and extremists continued to attack them. A kind of climax was reached in 1916 with the publication of Madison Grant's *The Passing of the Great Race*. Grant sounded impressive. He was chairman of the New York Zoological Society, trustee of the American Museum of Natural History, and counselor of the American Geographical Society. Henry Fairfield Osborn, research professor of zoology at Columbia University, wrote a preface for the book. The message? Simple, blatant racism. The Anglo-Saxons, or Nordics, were the supermen of the universe. The races drawn from the "lowest stratum of the Mediterranean basin and the Balkans" were "human flotsam." They were lowering the whole tone of America's social, moral, and political life. Grant and Osborn anticipated Adolf Hitler's Nordic madness by more than a decade.

A year after the publication of this vicious book, America was at war. This time, the war was not against the slaveholding South. It was an overseas war, against the nation which had sent more immigrants to the United States than any other—Germany. We were fighting on the side of our traditional enemy, England. Around the world, cynics predicted that America would never be able to summon its vast immigrant population to lay down their lives for a country they had only adopted. Others declared that the German-Americans would never bear arms against the Fatherland. There would be a revolution in the United States, led by Germans and those sympathetic to them, such as the Irish, who also hated England for the centuries of oppression the British had inflicted on their native land.

Until the moment the United States declared war, there was considerable support for Germany among German-Americans in the United States. Their love of German culture, the continuation, in many areas, of the old stockade mentality, made this inevitable. Then came a series of blows that shattered forever this sentimental attachment for the Fatherland. First, a careless German official left his briefcase on an elevated train in New York. An alert American Secret Service agent snatched it up and rushed it to headquarters. Its contents revealed a huge conspiracy against American companies that were selling war material to the English and their allies. The Germans were planning to foment strikes and blow up plants, trains, and ships. Some months later came another revelation. The British government handed over to President Wilson a telegram it had intercepted from Berlin. It was to the Mexican government, and it invited Mexico to join Germany in an alliance against America. As a reward, Germany offered to help Mexico regain Texas and other portions of the American Southwest. Finally, Germany announced it was going to wage unrestricted submarine warfare against neutral—which meant American—as well as Allied shipping. No honest German-American could defend this arrogant militarism, and the German *Kultur* stockade collapsed for good. When America declared war, German-Americans volunteered by the tens of thousands and fought heroically on the Western Front.

This same zeal to serve their adopted country was displayed by every other immigrant group. Particularly striking were the nearly half million immigrants called in the draft who had not yet been naturalized as citizens. Under the law, they had a right to claim exemption from military service. Virtually all of them voluntarily waived this right and begged to be drafted. Typical was the letter which a young Yugoslav sent to his brother from an army training camp. "I should feel ashamed to leave the army and go back to civil life. Indeed, how I love my young healthy life, and how I long to be free again, going my own ways without hearing the command of another. But alas, am I justified to think of my own liberty and happy life, when the moment is here and it calls on every young man to give liberty to others?"

Over 400,000 Italians fought in the ranks, collecting 103 Distinguished Service Crosses and suffering a full 10 percent of the casualties. Thus did the "steerage slime" prove they were Americans. Poles, Greeks, Hungarians, Jews, responded with equal fervor. A report of the provost marshal of the U.S. Army proudly declared:

The great and inspiring revelation here has been that men of foreign and of native origin alike responded to the call of arms with a patriotic devotion that confounded the cynical plans of our archenemy, and surpassed our own highest expectations. No man can peruse the muster roll of one of

*our camps, or the casualty list from a battlefield of France
without realizing that America has fulfilled one of its highest
missions in breeding a spirit of common loyalty among all
those who have shared the blessing of life on its free soil.
No need to speculate how it has come about; the great fact is
demonstrated that America makes Americans.*

Yet, in spite of this magnificent vindication of America's immigrant tradition, Congress, early in the 1920's, clanged shut
the Golden Door. Why? One reason was a kind of emotional
hangover left by the cynical peacemaking at the end of World
War I. The United States had fought "to make the world safe
for democracy." England, France, and the other Allies soon
made it clear that they were still dominated by their ancient
hatreds and greed for territory. Moreover, the American economy had slumped badly when it tried to readjust from war to a
peacetime pace, and many people felt that America's ability to
absorb more millions of newcomers was nearing the end.

But the Immigration Acts of 1920 and 1924 used a national origin system that was shamelessly based on the racist
doctrines of Grant and Osborn. Quotas for each country were
established according to the percentage of persons from that
country present in the United States in 1920. This meant the
English and other northern Europeans vastly outnumbered the
newer immigrants—from eastern and southern Europe—where
people were still eager to come. Great Britain, for instance,
never filled its annual quota of 65,361. In other countries of
Europe, huge waiting lists soon built up; 61,293 in Poland,
132,435 in Italy. Japanese immigrants were entirely excluded,
over the vigorous protests of the Japanese government.

To their credit, many immigrant organizations, such as the
German Steuben Society and the Sons of Norway, fought the

new immigration law. President Herbert Hoover too denounced it. But the combination of racism and postwar disillusion was too strong. For the next thirty years, the law was to remain on the books as America's official policy, limiting immigration in any one year to slightly more than 150,000 with the strong national origins bias. But the story of the American immigrant was by no means over.

The great depression of the 1930's reversed the immigration flow for the first time in many decades. For many years, more immigrants returned to their homeland than arrived. For the entire ten years from 1930 to 1940, the net increase was only 68,693. But the immigrant of these years was radically different from the immigrant of earlier decades. Most of them were Jews or anti-fascists fleeing Germany, Italy, and other nations which had fallen under the spell of Adolf Hitler's anti-Semitic

Polish immigrants in the waiting room of the American Consulate General in Warsaw, Poland, 1932. Many immigrants at this time were professional people, fleeing Europe because of intellectual rather than economic restrictions.

PUBLIC HEALTH SERVICE

Dr. Albert Einstein.

racism. More important, 40 percent of them were professional men. Some 25,000 were lawyers, doctors, artists, and Ph.D.'s, men and women of intellectual distinction who made unique contributions to American life. They included Albert Einstein, perhaps the greatest genius of the twentieth century, the man whose mathematical theories created modern physics; the great German novelist Thomas Mann; and the equally brilliant theologian Paul Tillich. Others were less famous but made large contributions to American life. Richard Courant was a professor of mathematics at the University of Gottingen. Dismissed by Hitler, he accepted an invitation to New York University in New York City, where he built the largest department of applied mathematics in America and made significant contributions to the American war effort during World War II.

Rudolph Flesch.

Then there is the saga of twenty-seven-year-old Rudolph Flesch, who fled Austria in 1933, when Hitler occupied that country. He worked as a stock clerk in a commercial book bindery, then obtained a one-year scholarship to the School of Library Science at Columbia University. He got a job at the Readability Laboratory of the American Association for Adult Education and did a doctoral dissertation, "Marks of a Readable Style." A few years later, he published his research in two books, *The Art of Plain Talk* and *The Art of Readable Writing*. Now a member of the guiding faculty of the Famous Writers School, this immigrant has taught Americans more about using their own language than perhaps any other single individual of our time. Today he gets inquiries from experts in Europe, asking for advice on how to simplify reading and writing in the languages of the Old World.

Among artists, perhaps the most famous refugee was Arturo Toscanini, the great symphony orchestra conductor, who was an outspoken foe of Mussolini's fascist regime in Italy. Toscanini accepted an invitation from David Sarnoff to direct a radio symphony orchestra which was formed specifically for him by Sarnoff's National Broadcasting Company.

Another Italian, Enrico Fermi, was the physicist whose breakthrough research enabled America to build the atom bomb. The hydrogen bomb was built under the guidance of Edward Teller, a Hungarian physicist, using data from the first modern computers, which were based on ideas of another Hungarian, John von Neumann. His knowledge of thought processes and of the brain itself led him to plan computers using as a model the human brain and substituting electronic tubes for brain cells. Von Neumann later became one of the five commissioners of

MEGGERS GALLERY OF NOBEL LAUREATES.
AMERICAN INSTITUTE OF PHYSICS

Enrico Fermi, winner of the Nobel Prize for Physics in 1938.

the U.S. Atomic Energy Commission, a remarkable tribute to the trust Americans placed in his judgment and genius.

Two giants of modern architecture, Walter Gropius and Ludwig Miës van der Rohe, both German-born, fled to America in the late thirties. Miës became chairman of the Department of Architecture at Harvard University, and Gropius director of the Department of Architecture at Chicago's Armour Institute, now the Illinois Institute of Technology. Hundreds of American architects were trained under them, and their influence on the buildings erected in the last twenty years in dozens of American cities has been immense. The Seagram building in New York, and many of the striking new apartment buildings along the lake shore in Chicago, were designed by Miës. Gropius designed Harvard's three-million-dollar Graduate Center and many private homes. In 1957, the American government chose him to design its embassy in Athens, only a mile from the Parthenon, where Western architectural history began.

Thus, by leaving the Golden Door open at least a crack, America reaped an enormous dividend on her historic tradition of offering asylum to victims of persecution and dictatorial oppression.

America's generosity to refugees did not close at the end of World War II. The plight of hundreds of thousands driven from their homes and living in wretched refugee camps in Europe inspired Congress to pass a Displaced Persons Act which permitted the admission of 200,000 DPs. Amendments to this bill enabled America to admit as permanent residents 387,244 of these desperate people. Other immigrants flowed around and over the quota system by the thousands. It has been estimated that from 1946 to 1957 about 2,600,000 immigrants entered the United States as non-quota persons, either as members of families already living in America or from South America and the West Indian islands, which had no quota limitations on their immigration.

When World War II exploded, finding America once more pitted against Germany, there were no longer any doubts about the loyalties of European immigrants. Only a tiny percentage of the German-American community had participated in Nazi propaganda in America or joined Nazi-oriented organizations, such as the German-American Bund. But Germany, unfortunately, was not the only enemy in this second World War of the twentieth century. America's entry into the conflict had been triggered by the destructive sneak attack on Pearl Harbor by the war planes of Imperial Japan. During the first year of the war, Japanese armies swept over the Philippines and other Pacific Islands, seized the British colonies of Malaya and Singapore, French Indo-China, and the Dutch East Indies, and menaced Australia. Japanese submarines surfaced off the West Coast of the United States and lobbed shells ashore. With the destruction of much of America's Pacific fleet at Pearl Harbor, the Hawaiian Islands seemed exposed to imminent conquest. Would California be next?

Although Japan already was fighting a war in China, and would obviously need years to digest the huge amounts of territory she had already swallowed in Asia, to some Americans the threat seemed all too real. It coalesced in their minds with the still-smoldering West Coast antagonism to the Japanese. On February 13, 1942, a congressional group recommended to President Franklin Roosevelt the evacuation of all Japanese from the West Coast. Even the prestigious columnist Walter Lippmann wrote a story implying that American military installations in Hawaii had been crippled by Japanese sabotage and that the same threat existed on the West Coast. The federal government ordered the FBI to investigate this and other reports of Japanese

WESTERN DEFENSE COMMAND AND FOURTH ARMY
WARTIME CIVIL CONTROL ADMINISTRATION
Presidio of San Francisco, California
April 1, 1942

INSTRUCTIONS
TO ALL PERSONS OF
JAPANESE
ANCESTRY
Living in the Following Area:

All that portion of the City and County of San Francisco, State of California, lying generally west of the north-south line established by Junipero Serra Boulevard, Worchester Avenue, and Nineteenth Avenue, and lying generally north of the east-west line established by California Street, to the intersection of Market Street, and thence on Market Street to San Francisco Bay.

All Japanese persons, both alien and non-alien, will be evacuated from the above designated area by 12:00 o'clock noon Tuesday, April 7, 1942.

No Japanese person will be permitted to enter or leave the above described area after 8:00 a: m., Thursday, April 2, 1942, without obtaining special permission from the Provost Marshal at the Civil Control Station located at:

1701 Van Ness Avenue
San Francisco, California

The Civil Control Station is equipped to assist the Japanese population affected by this evacuation in the following ways:

1. Give advice and instructions on the evacuation.
2. Provide services with respect to the management, leasing, sale, storage or other disposition of most kinds of property including: real estate, business and professional equipment, buildings, household goods, boats, automobiles, livestock, etc.
3. Provide temporary residence elsewhere for all Japanese in family groups.
4. Transport persons and a limited amount of clothing and equipment to their new residence, as specified below.

The Following Instructions Must Be Observed:

1. A responsible member of each family, preferably the head of the family, or the person in whose name most of the property is held, and each individual living alone, will report to the Civil Control Station to receive further instructions. This must be done between 8:00 a. m. and 5:00 p. m., Thursday, April 2, 1942, or between 8:00 a. m. and 5:00 p. m., Friday, April 3, 1942.

WAR RELOCATION AUTHORITY

A poster announcing the evacuation of all persons of Japanese ancestry from the San Francisco area, April 1, 1942.

disloyalty, and the Bureau, after extensive questioning of Japanese-Americans at all levels of society, reported they could find no evidence whatsoever to support the charges.

But the cry for evacuation continued. Typical of the kind of thinking behind it was that of another syndicated columnist, who wrote: "Personally I hate the Japanese." The governor of Idaho declared: "Japs live like rats, breed like rats, and act like rats. We don't want them buying or leasing land and becoming permanently located in our state." Others claimed without a shred of evidence that the Japanese were signaling to submarines offshore and directing their hit-and-run attacks.

In March, 1942, the army commander of the West Coast, Major General John DeWitt, ordered the evacuation of 110,000 Japanese. Seventy thousand of these people were women and children, 13,000 men fifty or older. Of the 27,000 other men, 16,000 were American citizens, 75 percent of whom had never seen Japan. Only 11,000 of them were alien men between the ages of twenty and fifty-five, and they lacked citizenship only because the law did not give them the privilege of naturalization. In his final recommendation to the secretary of war, General DeWitt said, "The Japanese race is an enemy race and while many second and third generation Japanese born on United States soil, possessed of United States citizenship, have become 'Americanized,' the racial strains are undiluted." By this kind of idiotic logic, it could have been argued that German-Americans were equally loyal to Hitler, and Italian-Americans to Mussolini.

Voices of sanity were lost in the war-inspired hysteria. The lieutenant commander in charge of Navy intelligence on the West Coast, a man who probably knew more about the inner workings of the Japanese-American community than anyone else, was not even consulted. Distinguished Americans such as phi-

Los Angeles residents of Japanese ancestry board a boxcar bound for the relocation camp in Manzanar, California, in 1942.

losopher John Dewey, who protested the decision as "race discrimination," were ignored. General DeWitt summed up the prevailing opinion when he told a congressional committee: "A Jap's a Jap. It makes no difference whether he is an American citizen or not."

Between March 24 and June 6, 1942, more than 100,000 Japanese evacuees were "processed" in 112 stations. They were placed in warehouses, fairgrounds; even the Santa Anita racetrack was pressed into service. Practically nothing was done to protect the property they were forced to abandon. The victims could only store their possessions in the basements of churches or farm outbuildings. Many were pressured by unscrupulous Americans to sell what they owned for little or nothing. Often these sharpsters would telephone first and say, "This is the FBI. This is just a friendly tip. You're going to be evacuated sooner than you think. You'd better get rid of your property before it's too late."

One Japanese who fell into this trap described the ruthless process:

Yesterday two men came. They said they were our friends "trying to be helpful." They did not even take their hats off, and kept cigars in their mouths in the room. "We will pay a fair price for your household goods," they said. "Thirty dollars for the washing machine, fifteen dollars for the piano, twenty-five dollars for the furniture in the dining room, twenty-five dollars for everything in the bedroom, seventy dollars for the automobile."

I had no one to move my furniture, there was no time to get enough help. . . . So I said yes, and they gave me a few pieces of paper money. I held them in my hand. So this was all our thirty years' labor amounted to. One hundred and sixty-five dollars.

Men who had served honorably as soldiers in World War I were included in the evacuation. Only Japanese who were in mental hospitals or tuberculosis sanitariums were permitted to remain behind. Several evacuees, overwhelmed by shame, committed suicide. One young man tried to get a plastic surgeon to alter his features, so he would not look Japanese.

Although most government officials were honest and did their best to treat the evacuees fairly and honestly, some were corrupt. One wealthy Japanese-American named Nomura was questioned day and night by U.S. Treasury officials, and was refused permission to leave his house, even to buy food. Finally he agreed to pay two of the Treasury officials 20 percent of all the money he made on his various properties. In one California county, persons entrusted with Japanese holdings were charged with stealing a half million dollars from them. An American Legion commander who offered to take over the drugstore of a Nisei friend simply sold it and pocketed the proceeds. When the U.S. government asked the Los Angeles district attorney to prosecute, there was "no interest in filing charges."

Finally, five months too late, on August 1, 1942, the War Relocation Authority took over responsibility for the evacuees' property, and moved what was left of it into government warehouses.

Meanwhile, the Japanese-Americans were moving to ten relocation centers in rural Arizona, Idaho, Wyoming, Utah, and Arkansas. In tarpaper shacks through which dust blew constantly, they tried to maintain some kind of civilized life. Doctors and other professional men were paid nineteen dollars a month. Skilled laborers got sixteen dollars a month, and most of the time they had nothing to do, as government red tape snarled promises of creating manufacturing opportunities in the relocation centers. Yet, in spite of this almost unbelievable mistreatment, the Japanese clung to their loyalty to America and begged for an opportunity to display it.

In the summer of 1942, the sugar beet growers of the mountain states suddenly realize that the army had depleted their available manpower. A bumper crop was about to rot in the fields for lack of harvest hands. Nine thousand Nisei volunteered and within a few weeks saved 915,000 tons of beets, rescuing 265,000,000 pounds of sugar, which was already being rationed because it was in such short supply.

The War Relocation Authority, under the leadership of Milton Eisenhower, was so encouraged by this achievement they began moving young Nisei out of the camps and back into colleges to continue their educations. Before the war was over, fifty-five hundred were in institutions of higher education, twice as many as in the prewar years. Others were moved to cities in the Midwest and East, where skilled-labor shortages in war industries were acute. In Chicago, where only 390 Japanese had lived before the war, 20,000 arrived and discovered, to their amazement, that there was none of the prejudice that had done so much to warp their lives on the West Coast.

Meanwhile, thousands more young Japanese-Americans kept volunteering for the army, only to be turned away. Then an army colonel, sent by Washington to visit the relocation camps, interviewed hundreds of these young men and returned to Washington convinced of their patriotism. He suggested creating a unit composed only of Americans of Japanese descent which would fight in Europe, where there was no reason to question their loyalty. Thus the 442nd Regimental Combat Team was born. After training in Texas, it went into action in Italy and soon achieved the most remarkable combat record in the history of the U.S. Army. Together with the 100th Infantry Battalion of Hawaiian Nisei, it accounted for 3,600 Purple

Japanese American members of the 442nd Infantry Regiment, in the Battle of Leghorn, Italy, July 12, 1944.

Hearts, 810 Bronze Stars, 342 Silver Stars, 47 Distinguished Service Crosses, 1 Congressional Medal of Honor, and 7 Presidential Unit Citations. General Mark Clark, who commanded it, called it "the most decorated unit in the military history of the United States."

Other Nisei, singly and in small groups, contributed their brains to the American war effort. They formed the teaching staff of the Military Intelligence Service Language School, where more than four thousand Americans learned to speak Japanese. Finally, Selective Service decided to take Nisei in the draft. Of the twenty-five thousand who were registered, no less than twenty-one thousand were inducted, a higher percentage than in any other immigrant group. They fought in the Pacific, as well as in Europe, without a single case of disloyalty.

In 1945, the government abandoned its exclusion policy, and the evacuees were permitted to leave their centers. Thanks to the heroism of their sons during the war, they found a drastically changed attitude in many places. They were able to abandon their little Tokyos and enter professions and industries which had hitherto been barred to them. Only two-thirds of them returned to the West Coast. The rest found homes in a dozen major cities. Today Nisei have graduated from West Point and Annapolis. San Francisco and Seattle have hired Nisei schoolteachers. Many Japanese now look upon the humiliating evacuation of World War II as the "helpful catastrophe."

11

SOME
SPANISH FLAVORING

In August, 1942, the *Los Angeles Times* ran the following headline:

POLICE SEIZE 300 IN BOYS GANG DRIVE

MANY WEAPONS TAKEN IN ROUNDUP CONDUCTED

BY HUNDREDS OF OFFICERS

Day after day the newspapers ran stories about "pugnacious Mexican youth . . . Weekly outbreaks of violence . . . Guerrilla gang warfare." Everywhere, throughout California, war workers, servicemen, and law-abiding citizens were soon convinced that their safety was threatened by a "Mexican crime wave."

Thus did another major immigrant group meet that old, familiar villain, prejudice. Mexican-Americans were in California before the Americans got there. They fought a brief, losing battle with the North Americans when the Mexican War broke out in 1846. After a few months under the flag of the "Bear State Republic," California entered the Union. Some Mexicans, such as Joaquín Murrietta, fought on for a while as guerrillas in the hills, but eventually they were hunted down and hanged.

Many of these early settlers returned to Mexico, but many did not. In 1910, there were an estimated 33,694 Mexicans living in California, and by 1920, the number had increased to 88,771. As California became America's greatest farm state, the need for laborers lured thousands of poor Mexicans across the border with that ancient immigrant desire for a better way of life. In Texas, thousands more poured in to work in the cotton fields; in Montana and Colorado it was the beet fields that drew them, and in Arizona the copper mines. By 1930, there were 368,013 Mexicans in California alone, and at least that many in Texas. By the time World War II began, there were close to 2,000,000 of them throughout the Southwest and West.

Along with their Spanish language and their preference for supposedly strange foods—*tortillas, enchiladas, frijoles*—they were Catholics in an area that was strongly Protestant. Worst of all, they were poor. Even today, agriculture pays the lowest wages in the country, and in the earlier years of the century, they were even lower (fifty-six cents a day). The Mexican farm workers lived in cars, dirty camp shacks, crowded tents without toilet facilities. Children as young as six years old went into the fields to pick fruit and cotton beside their parents. If the men struck for higher wages, they were threatened with immediate deportation to Mexico. Elsewhere, Mexicans found advancement repeatedly blocked for them. Foremen's jobs on the railroad went to Irish, German, and Italian sons of immigrants. One Mexican, who was working as a foreman's helper on the railroad, but getting laborer's wages, protested. The railroad fired him, then hired him back after he signed a paper surrendering his twenty-five years of seniority.

It is hardly surprising to discover that a Los Angeles city housing survey reported in 1939 that half of the Mexicans interviewed were living in overcrowded slums. In Texas, the housing conditions were even worse. A San Antonio housing survey reported 90 percent of the Mexican homes were below standard. When the Los Angeles County government built Aliso Village, a housing project, one little Mexican girl told what it meant to her family, by describing how she had lived before she moved into the modern apartment:

> *My family lives in a house where the rent is cheap but the house is bad. Never a bathtub and the family lived there fifteen years. My father fixed the house so at least we could receive some company. Before that we never invited any friends. Cockroaches came from the walls, bedbugs crawled on the beds. We had to sleep on the floor and breathed on each other. This is not very sanitary. It makes you tired to go to school in the morning. And if you have no bathroom in the house, it's hard to take a bath. . . . And with no toilet how can you be comfortable?*

Even worse were the hovels the farm workers built in the country. Few had running water, and garbage was thrown into the streets or into nearby streams. Even when a Mexican family built up a little capital, they found it difficult to find decent housing. "Restrictive covenants" kept them out of most decent neighborhoods in towns. A Mexican-American who had become a dentist tried to buy a home on the west side of Los Angeles, and was refused because he was "non-Caucasian."

One Mexican-American, Alex Bernal, fought back. In the

mid-1940's three neighbors—an oil-well driller, a salvage-store manager, and a garage owner—tried to evict him from a home he had bought in Fullerton, California. They testified that Mexicans were "dirty, noisy, lawless." Superior Judge Albert F. Ross smacked them down. "We are a country formed of people that come from other countries," he told them. "If it is decided that because a person is a Mexican he can be restricted from occupancy, the same rule will have to apply to the English, French, or anyone else that any residence district might see fit to exclude. . . . Mr. Bernal is not a Mexican according to our law."

Mexican-Americans have the traditional Spanish love of bright colors and stylish clothes. Among the lower-class young men in the slums, the fashion during the World War II years was the "zoot suit"—a costume identified by wide, ballooning trousers that were pegged tightly at the ankle, and a suit coat with heavily padded shoulders. It was popular with many city teenagers. But for the young Mexicans, it became a kind of defiant uniform which separated them from the North Americans, who discriminated against them.

Servicemen—sailors and marines and soldiers—from the many bases in California often wandered into the Mexican sections of Los Angeles, and when they ridiculed these zoot suits, almost invariably a brawl would result. For a while, the outnumbered servicemen got the worst of it. But when the papers began their anti-Mexican campaign, and the police began dragnet-style operations which arrested two and three hundred young Mexican boys and girls in a single night, the belief became widespread throughout the service camps that the Mexicans were vicious criminals who needed disciplining. Swarms of servicemen, often with the full approval of their officers, descended on the Mexican quarter of the city, and while the

Los Angeles police stood by and did nothing, they beat up very zoot suiter they could find. *Time* magazine called it "the ugliest brand of mob action since the (Chinese) Coolie race riots of the 1870's," but the local California press continued to treat these outbursts of violence as a joke. "Two hundred and eighty men sailed up the Los Angeles River early today and in a task force of taxicabs launched a reprisal attack on 'zoot-suit gangsters' in East Los Angeles," one reporter wrote.

Mexican-Americans were dragged from theaters, stripped of their clothing, beaten, and left naked on the streets. Then the police would arrive and arrest the victims for rioting. Again, the voices of sanity went unheard. Carl Holten, chief probation officer of Los Angeles County, declared, "There are probably between thirty-six thousand and thirty-eight thousand young Mexican-Americans in this county, and the recent gangsterism has not involved more than a few hundred." The Los Angeles County Grand Jury said that the "young people of Mexican ancestry have been more sinned against than sinning, in the discriminations and limitations that have been placed on them and their families."

The "zoot-suit riots" grew worse, until, in the early summer of 1943, an all-out melee finally engulfed most of downtown Los Angeles, with thousands of servicemen and civilians hunting down Mexicans in zoot suits. A general riot alarm was sounded, and a thousand policemen were thrown into the battle to suppress the violence, which was wrecking theaters, bars, restaurants, and even private homes. Los Angeles was finally declared out of bounds for naval personnel, and a Citizens' Committee gave Governor Earl Warren a report which blamed the police and the newspapers for creating the atmosphere of prejudice that encouraged the violence. "Mass arrests, dragnet raids, and other wholesale classifications of groups of people are based on false premises and tend merely to aggravate the situation. Group accusations foster race prejudices," the committee report said.

Ironically, Mexican-Americans from New Mexico—the 200th and 515th National Guard regiments—had proven their loyalty to their adopted country in the first year of the war. They had been sent to the Philippines only a few months before Pearl Harbor and were trapped there by the Japanese surprise attack. They fought heroically in the jungles of Bataan and on Corregidor and inspired tens of thousands of other young Mexican-Americans to all but storm the recruiting offices, begging for a chance to fight. No less than 375,000 of them served in the armed forces, and their casualties were far out of proportion to their numbers. In Los Angeles, where they formed about 10 percent of the population, 20 percent of the killed or wounded had Spanish names. Twenty-six Texans won the Medal of Honor during World War II. Five were Mexican-Americans.

The war gave the Mexicans a chance to take a great leap forward. One student of their problems says they advanced ten years in the four years that hostilities lasted. Manpower-hungry industries gave them jobs and promotions. The younger men returned from fighting and traveling around the world with vastly more self-confidence. In 1942, for instance, there were only fifteen Spanish-named students at Trinity University in San Antonio. By 1950, their number had multiplied fifteen times. The census-takers of 1930 could find only 1,100 Mexican-Americans who had qualified as teachers, only 165 physicians, and fewer than 100 lawyers. Ten years after the war, there were more than 16,000 in the professions, and that number has tripled since 1950. Mexican-Americans have also moved out of the Southwest. Toledo, Ohio, for example, has a Sociedad Mutualista Mexicana, a Mexican self-help society. Oc-

Cesar Chavez, the charismatic leader of the United Farm Workers Organizing Committee, surrounded by members of the organization, previously named National Farm Workers of America.

taviano Larrazolo has served as governor of the state of New Mexico, and Henry Gonzales recently won election to the U.S. Congress from Texas. Even more remarkable, perhaps, has been the emergence of Cesar Chavez as the organizer of Mexican farm workers in California and other Western States.

The presence of the Mexicans only serves to remind Americans of their historic debt to Spain. The word *cowboy* is a literal translation of the Mexico term *vaquero.* It was Mexicans who introduced Texans to the idea of raising cattle on the open ranges, and taught them how to use a lariat and branding iron, and the many other skills needed for successful ranching. Spaniards first discovered the copper riches of Arizona and other western states and developed the skills to get the precious metal out of the earth. Colorado, Nevada, Arizona, New Mexico, and California are full of the lovely, lyrical names the Spanish first wrote upon their maps. Many other words, such as *corral, bronco, rodeo, canyon, plaza, fiesta,* are considered English today, but were originally Spanish.

While the Mexican-Americans were finally achieving some recognition in the Southwest, another group of Spanish-speaking Americans were beginning their own immigrant struggle in the East. They came from Puerto Rico, an island wrested from Spain during the Spanish-American War. About one hundred miles long and thirty-five miles wide, it has a population of three million, and in 1947 the per capita income was $306 a year. The average income per person in the United States in the same year was four times that amount. Life was hard and poor in Puerto Rico, and as early as 1940, more and more of these islanders began coming to New York City. By 1957, there were 550,000 in New York City and another 175,000 in Chicago, Philadelphia, and other cities.

Inevitably, their very numbers created prejudice. One daily newspaper's headline in 1946 was, TIDAL WAVE OF PUERTO RICANS SWAMPING THE CITY. In 1948, when about 180,000 Puerto Ricans were in New York, another newspaper declared the real figure was 710,000. Actually, Puerto Ricans came to the city in a fairly steady flow from 1946 through 1960, at a rate of about 30,000 a year. But in 1961, when job opportunities sagged, there was a loss of 1,754, and in 1963 the loss went to 5,479. Many Puerto Ricans were discouraged by the harsh climate and the even harsher economic problems in New York. Their low wages forced them to live in some of the city's worst slums. Prejudice often took the form of violence.

On March 25, 1957, the *New York Post* carried a story headed: WE WERE TALKING IN SPANISH—AND THE WORDS MEANT DEATH. A Puerto Rican veteran just discharged from the army had stopped in a Brooklyn bar for a drink with his brother.

The other drinkers objected to their Spanish language and stomped the veteran to death.

In spite of such deplorable incidents, the Puerto Ricans have made remarkable progress in New York. One clergyman said in 1957: "No previous immigrant group so quickly numbered among its members so many policemen and welfare workers, teachers and social workers, office workers and independent businessmen, and even doctors and lawyers—after barely a dozen years in New York. And the signs of the future are in the substantial enrollment of young Puerto Ricans in the city's colleges and universities." A University of Chicago professor declared that the Puerto Ricans "may become assimilated as fast as the Italians, the Polish, and the Czechs have and much faster than the Negroes and Mexicans."

One reason for this is, probably, the eagerness of second-generation Puerto Ricans to become Americanized. One told an interviewer: "Most of my friends are Spanish, but we mostly talk English. When we talk to Spanish people we talk English to help them to learn to talk English."

At the same time, the nearness of Puerto Rico—only a few hours away by plane—has tended to make many Puerto Ricans simultaneously cling to their Spanish backgrounds. Each year, a million and a half persons travel between Puerto Rico and the American mainland, and most of them are native Puerto Ricans or second-generation Puerto Ricans "going home" to visit.

But the second generation does not share the first generation's dream of going home for good someday. To them, home isn't a dusty plaza on a tropical island, but a New York block where smells of fried fish and hamburgers mingle with the Latin beat drifting from the corner record store. More and more of these second-generation types are known as Mike and Manny rather than Miguel and Manuel and they often speak genuine Brooklynese, though they may retain a soft accent. They switch easily from Spanish to English as they talk to one another and to parents and friends. When they visit the old island, they often discover they are treated and feel like strangers.

"When I first saw Puerto Rico it was a culture shock," says a twenty-six-year-old radio announcer. "It was not very rural to me. It's not an enchanted island." He spent six days there visiting relatives and has no desire to return.

A Philadelphia report noted the "entrepreneurial superiority" of the Puerto Rican. This means they are willing to take the risk of starting their own businesses. Most typical are the *bodegas,* or Spanish-style grocery stores. In Philadelphia there was one in 1948. By 1956 there were forty; today there are over eighty. Throughout the country, it is estimated that there are at least four thousand bodegas and twenty-eight hundred other Puerto-Rican-owned stores, barbershops, and restaurants. A

A bodega on New York City's West Side. Hundreds of small Spanish-style groceries like this are to be found throughout New York City and its boroughs.

FRANK MAXWELL PHOTO

Herman Badillo, born in Caguas, Puerto Rico, came to New York at the age of eleven, graduated Magna Cum Laude from City College of New York in 1951, and Cum Laude from Brooklyn Law School in 1954. Mr. Badillo served as president of the Borough of the Bronx from 1966 to 1970, and he was a candidate for the Democratic nomination for mayor of New York in 1969.

New York study showed Puerto Ricans moving steadily out of the slums. By 1960 they were living in 74 percent of the city's neighborhoods. Many are already homeowners. They live in areas which extend from the eastern tip of Long Island across to the west shore of the Hudson and up into Westchester County. The same thing is happening in other parts of the country. *The Cleveland Press* quoted a well-known realtor: "A lot of Puerto Ricans plan to settle permanently and buy homes in the area. . . . We found them to be good financial risks, making their payments on time. They are becoming a credit to the community, although many of the old-timers protested when they moved in." By 1964, over five thousand Puerto Ricans held jobs in the city government of New York. Their first prominent public official, Herman Badillo, was elected President of the Borough of the Bronx for a four–year term in 1966. More than six thousand small businesses are operated by Puerto Ricans in New York. They are becoming doctors, lawyers, policemen, and firemen at a steadily accelerating pace.

Their attitude—pride in their Spanish origins, and a deep devotion to America—was perhaps best summed up on Columbus Day a few years ago, when they placed a wreath at the base of the statue of the Italian navigator in Central Park. With the wreath was a placard which read:

WE DO NOT KNOW WHERE
HE WAS BORN BUT WE DO KNOW
HIM AS A CITIZEN OF SPAIN
AND AS THE ADMIRAL
OF THE SPANISH EXPEDITION
IN WHICH THE NEW WORLD
WAS FOUNDED.
AMERICA WAS DISCOVERED
FOR THE GLORY OF SPAIN
AND THE GOOD OF ALL PEOPLE.

BY

HEWLETT & BRIGHT.

SALE OF

VALUABLE

SLAVES,

(On account of departure)

The Owner of the following named and valuable Slaves, being on the eve of departure for Europe, will cause the same to be offered for sale, at the NEW EXCHANGE, corner of St. Louis and Chartres streets, on *Saturday,* May 16, at Twelve o'Clock, *viz.*

1. SARAH, a mulatress, aged 45 years, a good cook and accustomed to house work in general, is an excellent and faithful nurse for sick persons, and in every respect a first rate character.

2. DENNIS, her son, a mulatto, aged 24 years, a first rate cook and steward for a vessel, having been in that capacity for many years on board one of the Mobile packets; is strictly honest, temperate, and a first rate subject.

3. CHOLE, a mulatress, aged 36 years, she is, without execption, one of the most competent servants in the country, a first rate washer and ironer, does up lace, a good cook, and for a bachelor who wishes a house-keeper she would be invaluable; she is also a good ladies' maid, having travelled to the North in that capacity.

4. FANNY, her daughter, a mulatress, aged 16 years, speaks French and English, is a superior hair-dresser, (pupil of Guilliac,) a good seamstress and ladies' maid, is smart, intelligent, and a first rate character.

5. DANDRIDGE, a mulatoo, aged 26 years, a first rate dining-room servant, a good painter and rough carpenter, and has but few equals for honesty and sobriety.

6. NANCY, his wife, aged about 24 years, a confidential house servant, good seamstress, mantuamaker and tailoress, a good cook, washer and ironer, etc.

7. MARY ANN, her child, a creole, aged 7 years, speaks French and English, is smart, active and intelligent.

8. FANNY or FRANCES, a mulatress, aged 22 years, is a first rate washer and ironer, good cook and house servant, and has an excellent character.

9. EMMA, an orphan, aged 10 or 11 years, speaks French and English, has been in the country 7 years, has been accustomed to waiting on table, sewing etc.; is intelligent and active.

10. FRANK, a mulatto, aged about 32 years speaks French and English, is a first rate hostler and coachman, understands perfectly well the management of horses, and is, in every respect, a first rate character, with the exception that he will occasionally drink, though not an habitual drunkard.

☞ All the above named Slaves are acclimated and excellent subjects; they were purchased by their present vendor many years ago, and will, therefore, be severally warranted against all vices and maladies prescribed by law, save and except FRANK, who is fully guaranteed in every other respect but the one above mentioned.

TERMS:—One-half Cash, and the other half in notes at Six months, drawn and endorsed to the satisfaction of the Vendor, with special mortgage on the Slaves until final payment. The Acts of Sale to be passed before WILLIAM BOSWELL, *Notary Public*, at the expense of the Purchaser.

New-Orleans, May 13, 1835.

PRINTED BY BENJAMIN LEVY.

A handbill announcing the sale of slaves in New Orleans, May 13, 1835.

⊰12⊱

BLACK
AMERICANS

THE FIRST NEGROES arrived in the United States from Africa in 1619, a year before the *Mayflower*. Yet in the long sweep of history covered by this book, black Americans have been mentioned only in passing. Why? Because the Negro is a double immigrant in American history. The vast majority of the black men who came to America during the first two hundred years were slaves, in chains. Most of them remained in slavery, uneducated and oppressed, until the Civil War. Even the minority —about 400,000—who managed to achieve freedom before the Civil War (and among those in the South, even owned black slaves themselves) were forced to live narrow, segregated lives. They were barred from most schools and colleges, denied the right to vote, and were severely limited in their job opportunities.

Yet more than 186,000 Negroes fought in the Union Army during the Civil War, and fought well. The war brought freedom to their 4,000,000 fellow Negroes still in slavery. For another decade the Federal government struggled to give educational and economic aid to this huge mass of destitute bewildered people. But the South was grimly determined to maintain white supremacy, and they saw their opportunity, when the Presidential election of 1876 ended in a disputed victory for the Republicans. Rutherford B. Hayes, the Republican candidate, could not become President without the electoral votes of three southern states, which the Democrats maintained had been stolen with the connivance of the Union Army, still stationed there. The Democrats had a majority in Congress, and threatened to filibuster which would have left the country without a President. The Republicans then made an historic agreement. They would withdraw the Union Army from the South and let the southerners deal with the Negro. Night riders, dressed in flowing white robes, and calling themselves the Ku Klux Klan, terrorized the blacks. In a few years the Negro was deprived of his vote, forced into a segregated society, and doomed to live as a sharecropper or fieldhand, not much better off then he had been under slavery, and in some cases worse.

Not until World War I, when a labor shortage developed in northern defense plants, was the Negro able to escape in any significant numbers from this harsh, repressive way of life. Chicago became the "top of the world." Within a decade, the number of Negroes living there doubled, to 109,000. More than 75,000 Negroes worked in the coal mines of Illinois, Pennsylvania, Ohio, and West Virginia. Another 150,000 were at work on the railroads. To die from the bite of frost is far more glorious than at the hands of a mob," wrote the *Chicago Defender,* a popular Negro newspaper. In 1917, the *Christian Recorder* wrote, "If a million Negroes move North and West in the next twelve months, it will be one of the greatest things for the Negro

MRS. WILLIAM HALLOWELL AND MRS. W. J. WOODIN

Henry Williams, First Sergeant, 1st South
Carolina Volunteers, during the Civil War.

since the Emancipation Proclamation." The census of 1920 showed that at least 330,000 Negroes had heeded this call to escape the South's repression.

But like other immigrants before them, the Negro collided with cruel prejudice. Not a little of it was spread by the Ku Klux Klan, which was active in the North and West, as well as in the South. Restrictive covenants—agreements between home-owners not to sell to Negroes—barred them from moving out of slums. When the National Association for the Advancement of Colored People persuaded the Supreme Court to strike these agreements down, whites in many cities resorted to another tactic—mob violence. The summer of 1919 saw no less than twenty-five race riots explode in American cities. For thirteen days mobs of whites and blacks rampaged through Chicago. Before the madness was over, 15 whites and 23 Negroes were dead, 537 persons were injured, and more than 1,000 families had been driven from their homes by fire bombs.

In Omaha, Nebraska, a mob dragged a Negro accused of attacking a white girl from the county courthouse, shot him more than a thousand times, and finally hanged him downtown at one of the busiest intersections.

But the Negro had tasted the free air of the North, and he was not going to allow violence to deny it to him. The steady movement north continued for the next two decades, and took a great leap forward in the years of the second World War. A million young Negroes were drafted, and at least another million moved north, to work in defense industries. Again, the progress was marred by race riots, both in army camps and in cities. Detroit in 1943 erupted in thirty hours of violence that killed twenty-five Negroes and nine white persons. The riot was sup-pressed only when six thousand troops were rushed into the city. After the war, the exodus from the South continued. In New

York alone, a million and a half Negroes entered the city—an increase of 250 percent in less than a quarter of a century. As Oscar Handlin, one of the best known historians of immigration, has pointed out, "This is a migration comparable in scope to that of the Irish and the Germans between 1840 and 1860 and the Jews and Italians of 1890 to 1915."

Poorly educated, and with few skills, these immigrants to American opportunity, if not to the land itself, have endured the harsh lot of previous newcomers to America's cities. For the Negro, the problems were complicated by the color of his skin, which adds mythical racist fears to the prejudice Americans have always displayed to the poor and uneducated. Another complication basic to the Negro American's problem has been the experience of slavery itself and the personal and psychological effects that this has had on both black and white people in this country. Also, the American business and industrial world was becoming more and more automated—machines were doing the work men formerly did with their hands—and this meant there were fewer job opportunities for the uneducated.

But the Negro also had an advantage, as the result of his black skin. He could issue a call to his fellow black men to join him in a massive attack on the problems that were blocking Negro progress. A. Philip Randolph, the Negro labor leader, and Walter White of the NAACP persuaded Franklin Roosevelt to ban discrimination in war industries and apprenticeship programs by threatening a march of 100,000 Negroes on Washington. In 1943, the Congress of Racial Equality was organized and staged its first sit-in demonstration in a restaurant in the Chicago Loop, protesting discrimination against Negroes. But no one saw the potentiality of mass Negro action as dramatically as a young Negro minister named Martin Luther King, Jr.

In 1954, the Supreme Court had banned segregation in

southern public schools. Extremist Southerners resisted with their usual tactic—violence. A dynamite blast destroyed Nashville's new Hattie Cotton elementary school, which had 388 white students and one Negro student. The National Guard had to be called out to escort small black children through lines of howling mobs in several towns in Kentucky and Tennessee. Martin Luther King, Jr., decided to respond in a new surprising way—nonviolence. "Love your enemies," he told the Negroes of Montgomery, Alabama, and led them into the streets in a series of marches and boycotts which forced the town fathers to abandon segregation on buses and in restaurants. Throughout the South, his tactics were used in city after city to fight segregation. Newspapers were flooded with pictures of police carrying sit-in demonstrators out of restaurants and libraries, churches and bus stations. It was the young Negroes especially who responded to King's leadership. A typical scene was enacted in a Tallahassee, Florida, jail. An agitated Negro mother offered to pay her sit-in daughter's fine, and get her out of jail. The girl told her mother she preferred to remain behind bars. "Mama, I love you," she said, "but I'm not free. And I'm not free because your generation didn't act. But I want my children to be free. That's why I'll stay in jail."

In the North, meanwhile, other Negroes began challenging *de facto* segregation—the result of whites abandoning neighborhoods to Negroes, and in effect turning the local public schools into all-Negro institutions. But it has been a long, slow fight, both in the South and in the North. In 1968, fifteen years after the Supreme Court outlawed segregation, only about one Negro child out of forty was attending school with white children in the South. De facto segregation in the North has actually increased, as more and more whites fled from cities to lily-white suburbs. The summer of 1963, the hundredth anniversary of the Emancipation Proclamation, was the high tide of the Negro nonviolent movement. More than sixteen hundred marches, mass meetings, and protests were held throughout the nation, with whites joining Negroes to show their support. The climax was reached on August 28, 1963, when more than 250,000 Americans—about 60,000 of them white—joined in a massive demonstration in Washington, D.C. Numerous speakers called for the immediate passage of a civil rights bill, and the end of segregation and prejudice against Negroes throughout American life. The speaker who evoked the deepest emotion was Martin Luther King, Jr.:

I have a dream that one day this nation will rise up and live out the true meaning of its creed: We hold these truths to be self-evident that all men are created equal.
I have a dream that one day on the red hills of Georgia the sons of former slaves and the sons of the former slave owners will be able to sit down together at the table of brotherhood. When we let freedom ring, when we let it ring from every village and hamlet, from every state and city, we will be able to speed up that day when all God's children, black men and white men, Jews and Gentiles, Protestants and Catholics, will be able to join hands and sing in the words of that old Negro spiritual:
> *"Free at last! Free at last! Thank*
> *God Almighty we are free at last."*

Eighteen days after the march, a car roared past the Sixteenth Street Baptist Church in Birmingham, Alabama. There was a tremendous explosion, and the old church crumpled into a chaos of smoke and flame. Four children died in the blast, and two young Negroes were killed later in the day in the rioting

Dr. Martin Luther King, Jr., with Mrs. King, shakes hands with Ralph J. Bunche, UN Under-Secretary-General for Special Political Affairs. Dr. King had just been awarded the 1964 Nobel Peace Prize. Mr. Bunche was awarded the Nobel Peace Prize in 1950.

Malcolm X.

that erupted throughout Birmingham. Although Congress passed an historic Civil Rights Bill in 1964, outlawing segregation in public facilities and setting up fair employment standards, the Negro masses were still imprisoned in the big-city ghettos by the immigrant's old foes—prejudice, poor education, and demoralizing living conditions. Out of this frustration, and in reaction to the violence wreaked on them so often in the past, huge riots have erupted in several American cities. In August, 1965, the Watts section of Los Angeles went up in flames to shouts of "Burn, baby, burn," and forty million dollars' worth of property was destroyed.

Watts is a good example of what the Negro is enduring in the slums. Twenty percent of the houses are dilapidated, and congestion is four times what it is in the rest of Los Angeles. Thirty percent of the potential Negro wage earners were unemployed at the time of the riot.

The following year, Detroit and then Newark were battered by similar riots. Then Martin Luther King, Jr., was struck down by an assassin's bullet in the spring of 1968, and violence exploded in dozens of cities. The era of nonviolent protest, aimed at achieving integration with white America, seemed over.

Some Negroes began calling for "Black Power" to combat "White Power." Among them were the Black Muslims, members of a religious and social movement founded by Elijah Muhammed. The Muslims denounced white society as corrupt and called on Negroes to separate themselves from it. One of Elijah's followers, Malcolm X, broke away from the Muslims and attempted to found his own movement. In his autobiography, which is one of the most important American books of the 1960's, Malcolm told how and why he joined the Muslims after leading a life of crime and then broke with them because he realized white men and black men must learn to work together. Eventually Malcolm was murdered by the Muslims. Meanwhile, other Negro leaders adopted the Black Power slogan. One was Stokely Carmichael, a Jamaica-born naturalized citizen. He interprets Black Power as a call for the Negroes to organize cooperative industries, stores, real estate agencies, and eventually build up a Negro economy that would be independent of the white economy, to give them genuine equality with white society. Other, more extreme leaders have tended to interpret the idea as excluding whites from their organizations. Thus we see the old stockade mentality of the immigrant reappearing in the Negro experience, for many of the same reasons. Negroes want to strengthen their solidarity in the face of a sometimes hostile white world; they want to foster pride in their own achievements and traditions. Perhaps all immigrant groups need this stockade, to survive the first harsh years at the bottom of the American ladder. As the American Negro progresses, the stockade will probably wither away, as it has done with other groups.

This may be sooner than some people think. Recently Phyllis Natalie Braxton, a Negro secretary from Washington, D.C., wrote the following article in *Glamour* magazine:

What's in a name? In a simpler age, tribes, each in its own vernacular, referred to themselves as "we, the people"; they named other tribes the equivalent of "everyone else" or for some tribal peculiarity. The Algonquians, for example, gave the Eskimos (Raw Flesh Eaters) their name. Who knows or cares today what the Raw Flesh Eaters called themselves? In the same vein, who cares what we call ourselves, we Americans of African descent? We know who we are. If other people don't, our insistence that they call us black won't help. And insistence that I call myself black won't help either, any more than it helped for people to correct me until I finally began to call myself Negro. As of now, I am colored, black, Negro, Afro-American, and I am also a lot of other things which I don't want to deny. So, if all those who need a name would settle on the word "American," I am sure that no one would object. After all, what one word could more accurately describe a people whose blood is mixed with the blood of probably every nationality that has set foot on this continent and whose hearts, minds, souls and lives are given over to making America live up to its promise of freedom and equality?

Too many white Americans do not realize how much Negroes have already contributed to American life. In New York's Harlem, one of the North's oldest Negro communities, a cultural "renaissance," as it was later called, began in the 1920's. Among the leaders was James Weldon Johnson, who published his *Fifty Years and Other Poems* in 1917. The title poem, written on the anniversary of the signing of the Emancipation Proclamation, made it clear that Negroes were determined to achieve true freedom and equality in America. In 1922, Johnson edited *The Book of American Negro Poetry*, which gave many more Negroes a chance to display their literary talents. In 1922, Claude McKay published *Harlem Shadows*, a book that placed him in the front rank of American writers. In poems such as "The Lynching," "If We Must Die," and "To the White Friends" he spoke with bitter pride and true artistic authenticity. Other Negro poets who attracted attention were Jean Toomer and Countee Cullen. Finally, from Missouri by way of Mexico, Africa, and Europe came Langston Hughes, who wrote poems, short stories and novels.

Walter White, the president of the National Association for

Countee Cullen was born in Baltimore in 1903. He won Phi Beta Kappa honors at New York University, where he completed his first volume of poetry, *Color*. He received his M.A. from Harvard and went on to write a novel and numerous volumes of poetry. He died in 1946.

the Advancement of Colored People, was also a novelist. His book *Fire in the Flint* was a stark, vivid tale of Negro life in the South. Two years later, *Flight* told the story of a young Negro woman light enough to "pass" for white and the emotional agony she experienced, torn between the white and black worlds. In 1929, White wrote *Rope and Faggot: A Biography of Judge Lynch*—a profound and shocking discussion of lynch law in America. Magazines such as *The Crisis* and *Opportunity* were filled with the work of Negro writers. A group of actors, calling themselves the Lafayette Players, created the first genuine Negro theater. A Negro musical revue, *Shuffle Along,* with songs such as "I'm Just Wild About Harry" and "Love Will Find a Way," ran for a year on Broadway. It was written and produced by Negroes. This was the beginning of a series of smashingly successful Negro musical revues which made stars of actors and actresses such as Florence Mills, Ethel Waters, and Bill "Bojangles" Robinson.

Negro painters also appeared. Henry Ossawa Tenner was acclaimed in Europe, and Laura Wheeler Waring became noted for her paintings of upper-class Negroes.

Gradually, the example of the Harlem renaissance spread across the United States. Poets such as Waring Cuney and Sterling Brown emerged in Washington, D.C. Frank Horne, a New Yorker who worked in Chicago, won prizes for poems such as "Letters Found Near a Suicide" and "On Seeing Two Brown Boys in a Catholic Church." Although artistic creativity sagged somewhat during the Depression years, the tradition persisted, and flowered again in the talent of Richard Wright, whose book *Native Son,* published in 1940, was a Book-of-the-Month Club selection and a best seller. Ralph Ellison's novel *Invisible Man* won the National Book Award in 1952. Today, Negro writers such as James Baldwin and John A. Williams are ranked with their finest white contemporaries. Lorraine Hansberry's play *Raisin in the Sun,* a moving story about the inner life of a Negro family, won the New York Critics Circle Award in 1959.

Other Negroes have contributed notably to American science and industry. Elijah McCoy was born in Canada, the son of runaway American slaves. He was granted more than seventy-five patents by the U.S. Patent Office in the late nineteenth century for various mechanical devices. His best known in-

vention was the drip cup which fed oil to moving parts of
heavy machinery. The tiny cup was so highly valued by
machinists they insisted on "the real McCoy." Dr. Charles Drew
was largely responsible for the development of blood plasma.
Jan Matzeliger invented the lasting machine, which revolutionized the American shoe industry. Granville T. Woods,
a New York electrician, introduced the third-rail electric system for the propulsion of trains, and John Latimer made the
original drawings for Alexander Graham Bell's telephone and
invented the carbon filament for electric lamps. Other Negroes
invented such diverse items as the potato chip, the golf tee, the
mop holder, and the player piano.

Greatest of all Negro contributions to American culture has,
of course, been music. Jazz is a combination of African rhythms
and the folk songs of Negro slavery, and it came boiling out of
New Orleans at the turn of the century to transform American
music. It has been the inspiration for Negro musicians, such as
Duke Ellington, and white musicians such as George Gershwin.
Its popularity has spread around the world.

Like other immigrant groups, the Negro has used the sport-
ing world to achieve instant recognition. During the segregation
era the great Jack Johnson won the World's Heavyweight crown,
in 1908. In the 1936 Olympics Negroes Jesse Owens, Ralph
Metcalf, Johnny Woodruff, and Cornelius Johnson were the
stars of the American team. The Olympics were held in Berlin,
and the racist ruler of Germany, Adolf Hitler, writhed in an-
guish to see these black Americans running, jumping, and
vaulting his supposed Nazi supermen into the ground. Then
came Joseph Louis Barrow, the son of poor tenant farmers in
Alabama, who fought under the name Joe Louis. He won the
enthusiastic admiration of all Americans for his boxing skill in
the ring and his good citizenship outside the ring. Perhaps his

Leontyne Price is one of the world's leading lyric sopranos. She made her Metropolitan Opera debut in *Il Trovatore* on January 27, 1961.

Jesse Owens breaks the tape in the second race of the 1936 Olympics in Berlin.

greatest moment was the day in 1938 when he strode into the ring against Max Schmeling, the German boxer who had knocked him out in 1936 and had become the idol of the Nazi race propagandists. Louis flattened Schmeling in one round and became a national, rather than simply a Negro, hero.

In 1945, Branch Rickey signed Jackie Robinson to a Brooklyn Dodger contract and the Negro at long last broke the color line in baseball. Many years before, John McGraw had tried to smuggle Negro Charles Grant into his Baltimore Orioles as an Indian. Grant's Negro origin was discovered and he was banned. For two years Robinson played for Montreal, the Dodgers' Canadian franchise, while sports experts predicted race riots and bloodshed if he was brought into the major leagues. Rickey ignored the prophets of doom and put Robinson into the lineup in 1947. Attendance records were broken in New York, Boston, Pittsburgh, and St. Louis, as Negroes flocked to see Robinson play, and the Dodgers won their first pennant in six years, thanks in no small part to Robinson's brilliant performance at second base. To everyone's astonishment, including his own, Robinson was named Rookie of the Year.

Since that historic breakthrough, so many Negroes have poured into baseball, and won fame as stars, that it would take a full page to list them. Superstar Willie Mays of the San Francisco Giants stands second only to Babe Ruth in the number of home runs. Pitcher Bob Gibson of the St. Louis Cardinals racked up record numbers of shutouts and strikeouts. Pro football and basketball have produced equally remarkable Negro athletes. Bill Russell of the Boston Celtics is certainly one of the greatest basketball players in the history of the game, with Oscar Robinson of Cincinnati and Wilt Chamberlain of Los Angeles not far behind him. In football, Jimmy Brown of Cleveland, Gale Sayers of Chicago, and Mat Snell of New York have achieved star billing.

In 1950, Harry Truman issued an Executive Order ending segregation of all kinds in the U.S. Army. This has been an historic breakthrough for the American Negro. Thousands of Negroes have found equality within the army, and learned skills and acquired educations which they have taken with them into civilian life. Some Negro units in World War I and World War II achieved good combat records, but others did poorly, largely because they were segregated, and their morale was low. In Korea and Vietnam, the Negro, fighting beside his white fellow Americans in integrated units, has proven himself to be their equal in the harshest test of all—front-line combat.

Although millions of Negroes are still trapped in the slums, they are making solid progress. Each year hundreds of thousands of them cross the poverty line into the lower middle class, buy their own homes, and move out of slums into better sections of the city and even into the suburbs. They want to move faster, of course, and they should move faster. They have had to wait too long to reach even the point where they can begin to pursue the happiness which America's freedom of opportunity should give all men. But they are moving. There are 584,000 Negroes in professional and managerial occupations, 385,000 skilled craftsmen and foremen, and about 233,000 in colleges and professional schools. Negroes own about two million homes. They manage huge financial complexes like the Atlanta Life Insurance Company and the North Carolina Mutual Life Insurance Company. There are numerous Negro millionaires. Robert C. Weaver, an American Negro, great-grandson of a slave, came up through government and politics to be appointed Secretary of Housing and Urban Development, and thus become the first Negro in any President's Cabinet. Thurgood Marshall recently became the first Negro to sit on the U.S. Supreme Court.

Jackie Robinson (center) is now chairman of the board of Freedom National Bank, Harlem's first Negro-chartered, Negro-owned bank. In this picture, William R. Hudgins, president of the bank, Mr. Robinson, and Rose Morgan, board member, chat with neighborhood youngsters about banking careers.

NAACP LEGAL DEFENSE AND EDUCATION
FUND, INC.

Associate Justice of the Supreme Court,
Thurgood Marshall.

A verse from an old Negro song which Martin Luther King, Jr., often quoted in his speeches tells better than anything else what is the status of the Negro today.

Lord, we ain't what we ought to be
We ain't what we want to be
We ain't what we gonna be
But thank God, we ain't what we was.

❦13❧

TO BE CONTINUED

ON OCTOBER 3, 1965, at the foot of the Statue of Liberty, Lyndon B. Johnson, the President of the United States, signed into law a new immigration bill. It declared that the government of the United States was determined to apply and practice our ideals of equality and freedom. Abandoned for good was the national origin system. Henceforth, the United States would admit 350,000 citizens each year from all nations on a first come, first served basis.

So the story of the Golden Door will probably continue, as long as America continues. Today's immigrants no longer creep off smelly ships. Most of them debark from modern jetliners, and they are met by well-organized groups, such as the American Council for Nationalities Service, who help them through the first difficult months in their new country. At the same time, America continues to open its doors to refugees. In the last ten years almost 500,000 Cubans have fled to the United States to escape the nightmare of Fidel Castro's Communism.

The new immigration law is in most essentials the one re-
quested by John F. Kennedy in his message to Congress on
July 23, 1963. There would seem to be no better way to end
the story of American immigrants than this, the triumph of fair
play and justice, won through the work and sacrifice of the first
Irish-American president. In his book *A Nation of Immigrants,*
John Kennedy said: "Yesterday's immigrants . . . have supplied a continuous flow of creative ability and ideas that have
enriched our nation. . . . The immigrants we welcome today
and tomorrow will carry on this tradition and help retain, rein-
vigorate and strengthen the American spirit."

APPENDIX

The Immigrant Record
(Since 1820)

Country	Since 1820	Peak Year
GERMANY	6,822,807	1882
ITALY	5,030,394	1907
IRELAND	4,699,064	1851
AUSTRIA — HUNGARY	4,282,823	1907
GREAT BRITAIN (England, Scotland, and Wales)	3,869,816	1888
CANADA AND NEWFOUNDLAND	784,763	1924
RUSSIA	3,345,161	1913
MEXICO	1,326,370	1924
SWEDEN	1,257,492	1882
AFRICA (estimated)	1,000,000	unknown *
NORWAY	846,012	1882
FRANCE	703,786	1851

* Although the US. banned the importation of slaves in 1808, the law was never well enforced, and an estimated 15,000 Negroes were smuggled into the country each year between 1808 and 1860

WEST INDIES	708,242	1824
GREECE	503,463	1907
POLAND	458,107	1921
CHINA	415,084	1882
TURKEY	369,122	1913
DENMARK	355,301	1882
NETHERLANDS	340,761	1882
JAPAN	341,463	1907
SWITZERLAND	331,463	1883
SOUTH AMERICA	339,056	1924
PORTUGAL	295,426	1921
BELGIUM	193,277	1913
SPAIN	193,043	1921
RUMANIA	159,784	1921
CZECHOSLOVAKIA	129,894	1921

Over 33,000,000 white Americans are still classified as of "foreign stock"—born outside the country or of at least one parent born abroad.

BIBLIOGRAPHY

Bennett, Lerone, Jr. *Before the Mayflower: A History of the Negro in America.* Chicago, 1962.

Benson, A. B., and Hedin, Naboth, *Americans from Sweden.* Philadelphia, 1950.

Bergmann, Leola N. *Americans from Norway.* Philadelphia, 1950.

Birmingham, Stephen. *Our Crowd: The Great Jewish Families of New York.* New York, 1967.

Blegen, Theodore C., ed. *Land of Their Choice: The Immigrants Write Home.* Minneapolis, 1955. Norwegians.

Brown, Francis J., and Rouček, Joseph S. *One America.* New York, 1952.

Corsi, Edward. *In the Shadow of Liberty.* New York, 1935.

Eaton, Allen H. *Immigrant Gifts to American Life.* Philadelphia, 1932.

Fermi, Laura. *Illustrious Immigrants: The Intellectual Migration from Europe, 1930–1941.* Chicago, 1968.

Franklin, John Hope. *From Slavery to Freedom: A History of Negro Americans.* New York, 1967.

Gavit, John Palmer. *Americans by Choice.* New York, 1922.

Griffith, Beatrice. *America Me.* Boston, 1948. Mexican-Americans.

Haiman, Miecislaus. *Poland in the American Revolutionary War.* Chicago, 1932.

Handlin, Oscar, ed. *Children of the Uprooted.* New York, 1966. Writings of second-generation immigrants.

Handlin, Oscar, ed. *Immigration as a Factor in American History.* New York, 1959.

Hansen, Marcus Lee. *The Immigrant in American History.* New York. 0000.

Hoff, Rhoda. *America's Immigrants.* New York, 1967.

Lengyell, Emil. *Americans from Hungary.* Philadelphia, 1948.

Lonn, Ella. *Foreigners in the Confederacy.* Chapel Hill, 1940.

Lonn, Ella. *Foreigners in the Union Army and Navy.* Baton Rouge, 1952.

Mallery, Charles Payson, *Ancient Families of Bohemia Manor.* Wilmington, 1888.

Mulder, Arnold. *Americans from Holland.* Philadelphia, 1947.

Musmano, Michael Angelo. *The Story of the Italians in America.* Garden City, 1965.

O'Connor, Richard. *The German-Americans.* Boston, 1968.

Padilla, Elena. *Up from Puerto Rico.* New York, 1958.

Pessin, Deborah. *History of the Jews in America.* New York, 1958.

Polish Day Association. *Poles in America.* Chicago, 1933.

Potter, George. *To the Golden Door.* Boston, 1960.

Rand, Christopher. *The Puerto Ricans.* New York, 1950.

Rischin, Moses. *The Promised City: New York's Jews, 1870–1914.* New York, 1964.

Ross, Edward A. *Old World in the New.* New York, 1914.

Senior, Clarence. *The Puerto Ricans: Strangers, Then Neighbors.* Chicago, 1965.

Shannon, William V. *The American Irish.* New York, 1963.

Smith, Bradford. *Americans from Japan.* Philadelphia, 1948.

Solomon, Barbara Miller. *Ancestors and Immigrants.* Cambridge, Mass., 1956.

Train, Arthur K. *The Story of Everyday Things.* New York and London, 1941.

Wakefield, Dan. *Island in the City: Puerto Ricans in New York.* New York, 1960.

Wittke, Carl F. *The Irish in America.* Baton Rouge, 1956.

Wittke, Carl F. *We Who Built America.* New York, 1964.

Wright, Louis B. *The Cultural Life of the American Colonies.* New York, 1957.

Wytrwal, Joseph A. *America's Polish Heritage.* Detroit, 1961.

INDEX

To the Hebrew Congregation in Newport
Rhode Island.

Gentlemen.

While I receive, with much satisfaction,
your Address replete with expressions of affection
and esteem; I rejoice in the opportunity of assuring
you, that I shall always retain a grateful remem-
brance of the cordial welcome I experienced in
my visit to Newport, from all classes of citizens.

The reflection on the days of difficulty and
danger which are past is rendered the more sweet,
from a consciousness that they are succeeded by days
of uncommon prosperity and security. If we have
wisdom to make the best use of the advantages with
which we are now favored, we cannot fail, under the
just administration of a good Government, to become
a great and a happy people.

The Citizens of the United States of America
have a right to applaud themselves for having given
to mankind examples of an enlarged and liberal
policy: a policy worthy of imitation. All possess
alike liberty of conscience and immunities of
citizenship. It is now no more that toleration is
spoken of, as if it was by the indulgence of one
class of people, that another enjoyed the exercise
of their inherent natural rights. For happily
the

the Government of the United States, which gives to bigotry no sanction, to persecution no assistance requires only that they who live under its protection should demean themselves as good citizens, in giving it on all occasions their effectual support.

It would be inconsistent with the frankness of my character not to avow that I am pleased with your favorable opinion of my administration, and fervent wishes for my felicity. May the children of the Stock of Abraham, who dwell in this land, continue to merit and enjoy the good will of the other Inhabitants; while every one shall sit in safety under his own vine and figtree, and there shall be none to make him afraid. May the father of all mercies scatter light and not darkness in our paths, and make us all in our several vocations useful here, and in his own due time and way everlastingly happy.

G. Washington

The famous letter by President George Washington to the Hebrew Congregation in Newport, August 21, 1790, in which religious freedom is laid down as a basic principle of the new republic.

THE SOCIETY OF FRIENDS OF TOURO SYNAGOGUE